Kaleidoscope:
Shapes and Colors
of Childhood

Bill Kraft

To my wife Karla without whose invaluable assistance, unfailing loyalty, tenacious dedication, and incomparable lemon meringue pie this book would not have been written.

You must know that there is nothing higher and stronger and more wholesome and good for life in the future than some good memory, especially a memory of childhood, of home. People talk to you a great deal about your education, but some good sacred memory, preserved from childhood, is perhaps the best education. If a man carries many such memories with him into life, he is safe to the end of his days. And if one has only one good memory left in one's heart, even that may sometime be the means of saving him.

Fyodor Dostoyevsky, *The Brothers Karamazov*

Contents

Acknowledgements

I wish to thank the following individuals whose contributions were an integral part of the book: Editor Mike Nistler at *Minnesota Moments*; Editor Allan Burke at the *Emmons County Record*; Artist/ Illustrator Lisa Webskowski; Illustrator George Kraft; Illustrator/ Photographer Karla Kraft; Elaine Frey for providing photos; Tom Kraft, Bob Kraft, Betty Lou Fischer, and Annette Dahl for their generous words of encouragement.

Spring

Springtime Has Broken

It happened at the end of the school term in the eighth grade. After a week of rain, clouds broke off from the sky like brittle pieces of candy to let in blue patches and bracing, after-the-rain air to rouse the new season to life. It was another spring on the plains of Strasburg, North Dakota, in the 1950s, and I had just been emancipated from school books, ink bottles and the vigilant eyes of teachers from whose mentoring and guidance my youthful spirit yearned to be freed. My young world became animated by spring, an elixir's promise of new life and the prospects of games and adventures far removed from the demands of school.

The first rain of spring, it seemed to me, was not like those humid rains of summer weighted with a heaviness that enervates your spirit and your energy. Spring rains came with the kind of air you wanted to quaff, to take in lung–filling drafts like your favorite ale at the tavern. It was a bracing air that shocked your senses to attention and shattered the long sleep of winter. Spring rains also left small ponds in our front yard, ponds which pricked my toes like icy thistles when I waded in them and embraced the soles of my feet with a frigid sensitivity almost excruciating in its intensity, a spring "rush" to announce the coming of the season. It was an invigorating challenge that always seemed freshest in the spring. Those rains also left in the sky bright columns of red, gold and green arched over the gymnasium at school nearby. I thought maybe it was God's way of wrapping the gift of spring in a rainbow of ribbons.

During spring sometimes new life arrived at the post office. That is where I first heard a wild chorus of chirping from behind the mail boxes. That chirping came from the young throats of chicks we had ordered for raising at home in the back yard. The chicks were packaged in cardboard boxes with holes in the top for ventilation. When the top of the box came off, rows of bobbing beaks and tiny yellow wings and feet floundered in a struggle for freedom. It was the kind of innocent desperation you wanted to relieve as fast as you could. Theirs was the innocence that comes with new life.

Spring also brought that redoubtable emissary of the season. The first robin. I anticipated his arrival with eagerness and regarded his appearance as the official coming of the season. I'm not sure we ever sang an anthem for spring, but if we had, "When cock robin comes, so does spring" would have been a fitting start. When he did appear, he did so prancing in princely fashion in fits and starts across the lawns, his red breast like the shield of royalty. For truly, the robin ruled the season like spring's good will ambassador. Even the mundane chores, the feeding of his family at the nest, assumed an air of elegance. Earthworms, nature's common morsels, in the beak of the robin, seemed almost like exquisite cuisine from nature's menu. When crows eat, we call it feeding. When robins eat, we call it dining.

With the advent of spring came games that we had so patiently anticipated during our long slumber in winter nights. The thaw of winter snow became small streams flowing down the streets into city drains. My imagination turned those streams into channels for adventures. The twigs I dropped into them became ships shooting the rapids on some grand mythological quest like Jason and the Argonauts in pursuit of the Golden Fleece. Perhaps I might encounter an angry god of the sea, Poseidon, with a wrath ready to capsize our vessel into the foaming waves and send us into the depths. Or maybe those twigs might become Huck Finn's raft on a river to new worlds of adventure and discovery. New worlds were only as far away as my fancies would take me. Young boys two generations later might take exception to my assertion that the technology of video games will never replace a young boy's greatest gift, his imagination, that wellspring of limitless possibilities that only he can tap. When video games manufactured by committee in the board rooms of corporate America occupy our imaginations, they become unwelcome tenants who crowd out our own resourcefulness. The sooner we evict them, the faster we grow.

Some games in spring have become synonymous with the season itself. Marbles is one of them. We played ours on the school yard nearby our house. There, on the playground still muddy with thaw, we drew circles and lines with sticks. The marbles we got from Keller's Hardware came in sacks of finely wrought net. Inside the sacks, marbles of blue, orange, and green bumped up against each other in our pockets. Years later the photos I saw of distant planets in astronomy books looked like the marbles I used to flick with my fingers. The blue sphere of Earth swirled with white or the red wink of Mars against the black infinity of space might have been the "shooters" I used to knock those marbles from their circles. Shooters were the big marbles we used to knock the smaller ones from the ring. Each player had his own preference. Some players preferred the big steel ones whose sheer weight seemed to be an advantage. The weight of the steel shooter provided greater force on impact and propelled marbles with a pinging sound out of the circles like planets breaking orbit into space. I never became proficient at the game of marbles, but some of my competitors honed their skills to near artistic perfection by somehow gripping the shooter between finger tip and thumb in a fashion that facilitated great accuracy. Those "top guns," the winners, collected their reward at the end of the game when they took your marbles home with them. I assume that the idiom, "taking all the marbles," has its origin in that all-American game from childhood. I never became a top gun, but maybe I should take comfort in knowing that my ineptitude at marbles helped secure "taking all the marbles" its permanent place in the lexicon of our native tongue.

Some of our spring fun required a bit more ingenuity and effort. The making of scooters presented a challenge. While the young girls roller-skated, we boys put roller skates to another use. We separated the skates into halves and nailed each half with its wheels to each end of a plank to form a running board of sorts. Then we nailed upright wooden orange crates from my father's store to the planks and nailed wooden handles of laths to the sides of the crates. The rider placed one foot on the plank and the other on the street and then pumped vigorously to get up to speed. While the scooter was functional enough, it could not be complete without some adornment. That adornment took the form of soda bottle caps we nailed to the front and sides of the scooters. Coca Cola, Pepsi Cola, Seven Up, Nehi Orange and Hires Root Beer caps glittered garishly like cheap trinkets in the noonday sun on scooters rumbling down the sidewalks. While such an obvious display of bravado probably impressed no one, we upped the testosterone stakes a bit on the sidewalk at Strasburg High School. There, the sidewalk ran a block long downhill from the school to the street. The precarious challenge of turning a sharp corner near the end of the walk might have dissuaded more sensible riders from attempting to negotiate it, but boys who yield to the caution of common sense have no fun at all. I suppose we should have taken heed from the roller skaters who had tumbled off the curve into the street to leave skin from elbows on the asphalt. But, of course, speed is a "high" and those of us who shot down that walk on scooters felt its crescendo when we approached the curve to the rumble of wheels on concrete and careened to the very edge of the walk. To my astonishment, I do not recall a single mishap of anyone who spilled over the edge. I cannot account for our good fortune, but if that daredevil of the wheels, Evel Knievel, had a guardian angel, I think he might have been working overtime.

Though our homemade scooters presented a challenge to our ingenuity, spring's thaw presented a more daunting one. The steep banks by the railroad tracks on the east edge of town filled the adjacent ditches with the spring run-off of melted snow. Barbed-wire fences that ran through the middle of the ditches might have snared swimming suits and the hides of anyone intrepid enough to enter the water. That is where the Bauer boys and I engaged in a one-upmanship of machismo-like derring-do. We dared each other to plunge into the numbingly cold water in the ditches. Until that moment, accounts I had read about cold's capacity to turn the skin blue had been but words on a page. Suddenly the reality of that cold seemed written in the marrow of my bones forever. When the cold became intolerable, we made for dry ground and trembling with cold fumbled and shook our way back into our clothes. If it had not been a test for the fainthearted, it had certainly been a test of the foolhardy. Boys with romantic notions of courage need to test their mettle. As King Arthur's Knights of the Roundtable had tested theirs in jousting tournaments in the days of yore, we tested ours centuries later in the ditches by the tracks. It wasn't as glamorous or as dangerous, but sometimes glories of the moment, even vicarious ones, are all we have. It is a contradiction, I suppose, that decades later I still feel a warm sentiment for that paralyzing chill down by the tracks.

Other swims in spring, though not always frigid, posed other dangers. Spring rains and thaws left shallow pools on the prairies, pools that became watering holes for cattle. When the nearest municipal swimming pool is forty-three miles away over gravel road, you sometimes make compromises with safety and sanitation. We compromised for the "old swimming hole" behind left field at the ballpark on the northwest edge of town. There I approached the pool on hands and knees and mud-crawled my way across. The sensation of clammy mud oozing between my fingers was interrupted by a stabbing pain in my left hand just below the palm. Jack Daniels was supposed to be found on the shelf in a liquor store, not on the bottom of a shallow pool on the prairie. The broken whiskey bottle had opened a gash to the bone. I clamped a hand over the small geyser of blood spurting from my wound and headed for home and first aid before that geyser turned into Old Faithful. Over the years the scar I got from Jack Daniels became the indelible mark of an innocent recklessness I regard with affection.

As for Jack Daniels, I decided to leave him on the shelf forever.

The gash I suffered was not the only consequence of my visits to the old swimming hole. Watering holes do not come with sanitary safeguards. Which means rash is inevitable. When mine erupted on the trunk of my body, I turned to the wisdom and medical lore of my mother whose home remedies would never find their way into the ER of the modern hospital. We called her remedy "schvevel," a mixture of sulfur powder and vegetable oil with an odor to offend even the hardiest of nostrils. Considering the alternative, we pinched our noses and took our medicine as loving hands applied it to the affected areas. And it worked! Only a mother could turn such an olfactory assault on the senses into the sweet smell of success.

With the season of spring came the season of Lent, that spiritual time of self-denial in preparation for Easter Sunday. In keeping with the practice of our faith, we bowed to the dictum that no meat was to be consumed on Fridays, especially during Lent. Anyone who ever dined on my mother's salmon patties and macaroni and cheese at Friday dinner might well have thanked the Lord for that delicious "sacrifice" of meatless meals. The taste of macaroni with butter-soaked bread crumbs and cheese bubbling up to the edges of the pot made roast beef seem superfluous. When the pot was almost clean, I scraped the butter-crust from the sides and bottom of the pot and voraciously consumed it. Years later I was tempted to facetiously observe that if man does not live by bread alone, maybe macaroni and cheese will suffice. It's the sort of benevolent sacrifice that might make converts.

In keeping with the spirit of self-denial, we children were expected to do our part. It was common practice at the time that children forgo treats during Lent. That is why we hoarded candy bars and assorted sweet treats in cigar boxes from my father's store. Those cigar boxes lined with intricate designs and colors of yellow and black seemed like exotic jewel boxes fit for treasures only. Indeed, the Hershey's, Walnut Crush and Powerhouse bars we crammed into the boxes became our jewels of sweet delight. On Easter Sunday we tore open the boxes and ravenously fed on our hoarded treasure. Until satiety became excess. After the third or fourth Hershey bar, sweetness seems less sweet. That was when the virtue of self-denial became the vice of gluttony. However, the satisfied smiles on our faces streaked with chocolate and caramel seemed like a good trade-off. Children can be forgiven if moral nuances are beyond their grasp. Such matters are best left to adults. The moral complexities of adulthood can wait while children have fun growing up.

According to family lore, that same moral complexity also eluded one of my brothers, who one Easter many years ago, placed a wash tub under his bed in place of the traditional Easter basket. When he found but one egg in the tub at morning, I assume he became enlightened by the obvious moral. Greed is not a vice to be cultivated, especially during the holy season of Easter. No doubt the lesson served him well. With all due bias, I assert that he turned out to be quite virtuous, indeed.

Other lore also attended the season. My siblings tell me of the time they let a rope down the upstairs porch on the south side of the house to facilitate the Easter Rabbit's access to our Easter baskets in the hallway. I never witnessed the Easter Rabbit's ascent on the rope, but somehow the prospect of a bunny climbing a rope began to confirm my doubts about the existence of the rabbit himself. Of course, the Easter Rabbit is like Santa Claus. You believe in the spirit of him, not his literal existence. It's not so much a loss of innocence as the conviction that what the imaginary represents is very real, indeed.

More of that lore took hold over the years when rumors began to flow that my friend Mickey Schmaltz had seen the Easter Rabbit trudging with a bulging basket of eggs down by the railroad tracks and grain elevators on the east edge of town. Any initial skepticism

I might have harbored began to dissipate when additional reports of similar sightings caught my ear. As with all legends, the embellishments that grow with them almost begin to assume the possibility of reality. And yet that rabbit always seemed to be tantalizingly out of sight. In fact, he remained out of sight for so long that doubt soon replaced tenuous credibility. Rabbits that can't climb ropes don't go walking down by the tracks either. Soon he became relegated to those mythological figures so much an essential part of our religious and cultural heritage. Yet I'm still not ready to dismiss him entirely. After all, the imaginary is sometimes the most real of all.

Sometime during Holy Week we dyed the eggs. My mother boiled the eggs while we opened packets of egg dye. The packets came with assorted discs of dye and a looped wire with a handle to hold the eggs while dipping. At times, we indulged in some aesthetic experimentation by dipping the eggs into a variety of dyes. The result often turned into an eclectic mix of the bizarre, a psychedelic clash of reds, greens, blues, orange and purple splashed on eggs. The results were a matter of personal preference. Conservative taste would have chosen the eggs of solid red or green while more adventurous taste would have chosen the "psychedelic egg." If eyes have a way of remembering colors, noses have a way of remembering smells. Sometimes I think my nose still feels the acrid sting of vinegar with egg dye in the bottom of a bowl.

Secular aspects of the Easter season gave way to the solemn significance of Lent and Holy Week at Sts. Peter and Paul's Church. Indeed, the season became colored with shades of purple, black, and white, each hue a symbolic underpinning of religious themes. Purple drapes during Lent covered the main and side altars with a muted aura of penitence, a somber prelude to the joy of Easter Sunday. On the side altar, the faces of Mary and Joseph remained veiled and ready to burst forth with an incandescent joy on Easter Sunday morning. On Good Friday, the black chasuble, a garment flung over the head and resting on the chest of the priest, seemed to cloak in darkness the heart of Jesus in his atonement for the sins of humankind. The liturgy of Holy Saturday, a three-hour marathon of blessings and chants, defined for impatient children the meaning of eternity. Fortunately, for the restive faithful, the Holy Saturday liturgy has long since been abridged, and I daresay that the new "Reader's Digest" version has found favor in the flock.

On Easter Sunday morning the purple cloaks were stripped from the altars while the black chasuble was replaced by a radiant white in glorious celebration of resurrection and new life at Easter Sunday Mass. Because the holy hues of Easter remain as vivid as my faith is strong, I don't think I'll ever see the colors fade.

After Easter Mass, families gathered in celebration at traditional meals. Slices of braided sweet bread brown-tinged under slabs of smoked ham filled the plates. My mother, as she did at Christmas, baked the ham inside a crust to seal the juices. I suppose it was the natural way to marinate, and maybe that is why no ham I've tasted since piques my palate in the same way. Delectable as the ham was, it was my mother Agatha's "rivel" soup that brought the children and grandchildren back for more a generation later. Saturday night became rivel night while my mother pinched hardened homemade dough into small pea-sized ovals. On Sunday morning the rivels were dumped into a chicken broth and boiled until firm or al dente. It was basic, but it was even more unforgettable. The revered rivel soup remains a staple in the diet of the German-Russian culture, its place at the very summit of culinary perfection.

With the passing of Easter in the spring, came that inevitable transition for young people, high school graduation, the moving on from the sheltered comfort of home and school to the "real world" outside. By my senior year, the uncertainty and anxiety of what lay ahead were already upon us. Maybe that is why our superiors at school felt obligated to schedule a commencement speaker who would, no doubt, get us off to an enlightened start. I suspect that Daniel Webster himself would have found the challenge a bit daunting. When the speaker at some climactic point in his address exhorted us to "Wake up, Little Susie," I was not sure whether he was referencing the current pop song, "Wake Up, Little

Susie," to jar us from our preoccupation with post commencement parties or sounding a broader call to arms for us to meet our new world with courage and direction. I was always skeptical about the effects of that speech. Somehow, for high school seniors, bombastic rhetoric lacks the tantalizing immediacy of pizza and girls after the ceremony. Whatever his intentions, the prospect of parties and Mickey Schmaltz spotting the Easter Rabbit down by the railroad tracks stayed with me long after those words had faded from the stage of Strasburg High School. The passing years have confirmed what I suspected at the time. Pedantic pomp is no match for good memories of childhood. Next time I'm home in the spring, I'll stop by the railroad tracks just to make sure.

Clock, Lakeside Drive-in

Time Warp in Big Lake

Have you ever had the feeling you were about to enter a time warp? That sentiment is not exclusive to *Star Trek* fans. A sense of déjà vu is likely to transport you to another time the moment you enter the Lakeside Drive-in in Big Lake, Minnesota. Located just off Highway 10, midway between St. Cloud and the Twin Cities, lies a quaint sanctuary for anyone looking to find the kind of ambience known to a generation of sock-hoppers as the 1950s drive-in.

Like a siren to those ancient seafarers of mythology, the Lakeside's neon-lit ice cream cone blinking in the window invites you to make port and sample its wares. It was a rendezvous that beckoned me the first time I spied a familiar orange and white structure along the roadside. The Lakeside Drive-in still retains some of the familiar trappings of its former affiliation with the A & W franchise and its signature look.

My stop there was almost mandatory since I had promised my companion, Karla, her first acquaintance with a genuine banana split. That rite of passage, such a universal fact in the life of the American teenager, had somehow eluded her during her formative years and had to be redressed.

Most conspicuous on the Lakeside's exterior are the old-fashioned menus that stand at eye level for the convenience of the drive-in customer. The menus are framed rectangular shapes against steel poles that prop the roof in a sort of canopy that hangs over the main entrance.

The moment you enter the Lakeside Drive-in, you are taken with its retro charm. The brown vinyl booths are designed for soft comfort. Phones resting atop the booths make ordering a novel convenience, while the yellow and red plastic condiment dispensers look as if they might still bear Fonzie's fingerprints. Squeeze them and they blurt out sudden pools of mustard and catsup all over your sandwich.

One piece of eye-catching ambience on the wall is the old clock with its miniature murals of 1950s Americana. On one mural, fins jut from the fenders of hotrods with enough macho horsepower under the hood to do justice to a James Dean drag race. On another, a teenaged boy perched on a spin-stool slurps a malt. On yet a third, a middle-aged couple at a table sits under a ribbon of streaming red letters that spell Coca Cola on the sign above them. The clock is stamped with the A & W logo against a pale blue.

Lakeside Drive-in Jukebox

The Lakeside's most affecting charm, however, is something no self-respecting retro establishment would be without. Its jukebox. This one sports the kind of garish sentimentality endearingly rooted in a time of simple joys. A rainbow of red-purple-orange runs up its front to form columns of inverted U's sprinkled with flashing lights that wink incessantly. Its square, box-like shape sits up against the wall in front of the service counter.

The selections on the jukebox appear on a white plastic panel that glitters like ivory keys on a piano and offers a vintage menu of 1950s rock classics from Buddy Holly's *Peggy Sue* to the

19

Richie Valens *La Bamba* and the Fats Domino *Blueberry Hill.* Rock icons included in the selections represent a virtual rock and roll Hall of Fame. It's a bargain, too. For a quarter you get two plays. For fifty cents you get five. For a dollar you get ten.

When the menu comes, it is brought by a waitress equipped with the tools of the trade. A change belt in a wide brown band is strapped to her waist. Metal cylinders that hold your change send nickels, dimes, quarters and pennies clinking into her hand when she pushes the lever at the bottom. It's the sort of quaintness you never see at the computerized checkout in your local supermarket.

We chose the Banana Split Royal from a menu that offers the staples of the American teenagers' diet of corn dogs, burgers, fries, root beer and assorted ice cream flavors. The Banana Split Royal meets your expectations. This royal treat is no misnomer. It comes near to overflowing in a plastic banana boat. Clouds of whipped cream, strawberry sauce, pineapple chunks and rich chocolate syrup ooze their way over scoops of strawberry, vanilla and chocolate ice cream that split the banana right to the edges of the dish.

The two plastic spoons that came with it soon became weapons in a friendly duel to see who could devour the treat more quickly. Maybe the male appetite is more formidable. Or maybe the frenzied rhythms of Jerry Lee Lewis's *Great Balls of Fire* propelled my appetite into hyper drive. Whatever the reason, the duel soon became a route. Karla's appetite was no match for mine.

Still, Karla had gotten her first taste of a "real banana split." If it took a sense of déjà vu to get it, so much the better. I know that somewhere "The Fonz" with his inimitable swagger is giving us the big thumbs up.

Summer

Sojourn in the City

It is a common truism that the only permanence is change. Sometimes change lies in wait for events to grab life and shake it topsy-turvy to see what falls out. Such changes alter your view of the world.

On the plains of Strasburg, North Dakota, in the early 1950s, I was about to embark on a journey to a world much broader than the one I knew. The provincial confines of my rural America were about to be shattered.

The first hint of it came with a ritual that always portended some grand adventure or the approach of a special holiday. At such times my father sent me to get a haircut at the barbershop across the street. There Jake Schreiner practiced his craft with a knowing hand amidst rainbow-colored prisms of bottled oils and tonics crowded onto the shelf behind his barber's chair. That chair behind the window in Jake Schreiner's barbershop also became my vantage point. Before me, Smalltown, America, passed by on its daily business down Main Street. Soon another window to another world would open for me. My father, part owner of Kraft Brothers general store, was going on his annual buying trip, and I, at the age of twelve, was going with him. To the big city. Minneapolis.

The journey that summer began with the 120-mile drive to Aberdeen, South Dakota, to link with the night train to Minneapolis. Our old '49 Ford was not the pride of the Ford Motor Company. Its only renown came from its inclination to go into vapor lock, thus making even the slightest demands on its reliability an adventure. That is why my father, always disinclined to get behind the wheel, prevailed upon one of the neighbors to do the driving. The gravel roads, pockmarked with holes, rattled the car with vibrations almost enough to shake it to rubble.

In Aberdeen we boarded the Hiawatha for my maiden journey by train. The train began to move first in sudden lurches and then in a steady rhythm of acceleration. On the tracks a faint murmur of a rumble rose and then became a roar as the engine sent the train in an onward rush toward the city.

Inside the train, sleep seemed like an intrusion. I pressed my face to the window to see the small towns pass by in a blur of lights that flashed and vanished like plumes of smoke. Maybe the night seemed to make the world go faster. Lakes and ponds that shimmered columns of moonlight shot by almost faster than the eye could see. I stayed at the window until exhaustion sent me to my seat and a restless sleep filled with anticipation for our destination in the morning.

My father always made reservations at the Andrews Hotel on

Hennepin Avenue. At the hotel the bellhop collected our luggage for delivery to our room. It was my first encounter with ethnic diversity. The bellhop was African-American. Unfamiliar with the common practice of tipping, I reached out to shake his hand. In gracious compliance, he reached out to join mine. Then I yielded to a sudden impulse. I looked at my hand for traces of black. It was the kind of naiveté and inadvertent transgression that would have been unpardonable in a time of different social sensibilities.

The Andrews Hotel came with the usual comforts and something else. A coin-operated black and white television set. A clink of a coin flickered to life the images of Stan Laurel and Oliver Hardy. In rapt fascination I watched them engage in one of their usual imbroglios. Laurel, pinned behind a post, his limbs all awry like some lopsided scarecrow, struggled in futile frustration in an attempt to extricate himself while Hardy, the benevolent bully, berated him for embroiling them in yet "another fine mess." Maybe that image still remains with me because it was my introduction to the wonders of a technology that had not yet arrived on the prairies of North Dakota.

The passenger elevator at the Andrews Hotel also provided another novelty. My first ride in an elevator. Automation had not yet replaced the human element, the elevator operator. The operators at the Andrews Hotel brought a certain dignity to their duties. Dressed in uniforms with stripes running down the legs and adorned with an assortment of gold buckles and buttons, they carried themselves with a bearing of authority. The sensation of motion during the elevator's ascent and its abrupt stop was followed by a curt but courteous announcement that we had reached our destination. It was conducted with the kind of comportment of men who took pride in their work.

Night brought little sleep. On Hennepin Avenue the steady din of traffic, the wailing of sirens and the sound of rubber left on the pavement kept sleep at bay. Still, they seemed like a minor inconvenience. I wanted the morning now. I wanted to see the city.

The skyline in downtown Minneapolis dwarfed anything I had seen before. The grain elevators in my hometown suddenly seemed scaled down, shrunken to miniatures. Towers of stone, glass and steel extended skyward forcing me to crane my neck to see the top. One of those structures was Minnesota's version of the Empire State Building. It was the Foshay Tower.

Even trips with my father to the retailers like Butler Brothers turned into small adventures. What might have been a tedious foray into a business world beyond my comprehension turned into another discovery during lunch hour. In a department store downtown I watched shoppers who appeared to be standing still somehow rise to another level of the store. They were not defying the laws of gravity. They were riding escalators. Flat surfaces of metal sprang from the floor and unfolded to become steps. My first attempt to mount one almost sent me into a free fall that was frightening and exhilarating.

More delights awaited me at Bridgeman's Ice Cream Parlor downtown. Adjacent to the Gopher Theater, Bridgeman's glittering glass façade was a conspicuous invitation to enter and partake of an eye-popping menu that included the La La Palooza, the Hot Fudge Marble Sundae, the Triple Treat, and the Turtle among its lengthy list of temptations. Long, sleek walls ran deep to the far end while in front rotating stools stood before the counter. I seated myself in one of the booths with the hard marble tops and metal dispensers that bulged napkins into the palm of my hand. Then I chose something with thick waves of caramel and nuts that crunched into a savory sweetness I hoped would last forever. Nothing back home was remotely comparable.

For finer dining my father took me to the renowned Forum Cafeteria on Seventh Street. To my undiscerning eye, the Forum was elegant in both its ambience and its cuisine. Its plush interior on two floors might have rivaled the opulent extravagance of a Hollywood set. Its choices of entrees, so numerous and so enticing, confounded me. How could I choose from so many riches? I could not have imagined that even the most fastidious of connoisseurs would have found cause to carp over its flawless cuisine. I, however, who thought that culinary perfection came in the form of a hamburger and fries, settled for the Salisbury steak and mashed potatoes.

Forum Cafeteria and Century Theater, Minneapolis, Minnesota

The city offered something else that stirred my senses. Splendid movie theaters. One of them was the Orpheum. Entering the Orpheum was somewhat akin to peering into a deep cavern. Rows upon rows of seats on the main floor numbered enough to swallow the entire population of Strasburg, North Dakota. Winding stairways with thick carpets led to a balcony that hung over the main floor.

At the Century Theater at 40-42 Seventh Street South, Hollywood's answer to the encroaching threat of television was called Cinerama. A screen divided into three sections projected images with startling clarity and grandeur. It was a technology ideally suited for travelogues and large-scale westerns that could make waves of stampeding bison seem to sweep in a downward charge right into your seat.

Aqua Follies at Theodore Wirth Pool, Minneapolis, Minnesota, 1940

Another excursion with my father took me to Theodore Wirth Pool, the site of the city's Aqua Follies in North Minneapolis. Towers on both ends flanked the pool to become launching points for Aquatennial divers at exhibitions for the public. My only previous exposure to anything comparable came from books and film. In a series of swan dives, flips and complex somersaults the divers split the water with arrow straight precision that left barely a ripple in the pool. Then teams of swimmers, undulating with swan-like elegance, their heads and limbs in perfect synchronization, executed their complex routines. It was a dazzling repertoire of grace and agility that left me in awed appreciation.

I have often returned to Minneapolis in recent years to avail myself of the finest the city has to offer. The city has changed. The Gopher Theater, Bridgeman's, the Century Theater and the Forum are gone. The Andrews Hotel, having fallen into disrepute over the years, was razed and replaced by a parking lot.

Sometimes a sentimental tug tries to pull me back to that other time so long ago. Yet I know that the Minneapolis of half a century ago was not the end of a world for me. It was the beginning of a new one.

The National "Past Time"

There was, in my hometown, a structure common to the small towns scattered across the Great Plains during the decades of 1940 to 1960. It was the local ballpark or "baseball diamond" as we referred to it. These structures were a matter of community pride less for the manner in which they were built than for what they represented. They became a repository of a town's competitive spirit and, on Sunday afternoons, the scene of spirited rivalries among the neighboring towns.

The local ballpark was distinguished by its most prominent feature, the grandstand. Ours, in shades of dark green, was propped on the north edge of town where the encroaching prairie grass intruded just enough to mark the demarcation point between well-groomed lawns and the rough edges of the prairie. It stood imposingly against the harsh elements of the passing seasons perhaps in tribute to the sturdy character and resourcefulness of the hardy German-Russian inhabitants who had built it. Its roof was propped up on wooden pillars deeply embedded into the ground and rising to a height that slanted downwards from the front to the rear. Presumably, the angle was to facilitate drainage of thawing winter snows and rains.

The roof served another purpose as well. On cold afternoons our childhood imaginations transformed that roof into a launching pad for our gambols in the winter snows. Deep drifts of snow carved by the winds into white waves became an ocean of snow into which we propelled out bodies from the top of the grandstand. We reached the top of the grandstand by scaling a network of X-beam supports that ran from the base of the structure to its roof. With an agility peculiar to childhood coordination, we climbed in sudden lurches from beam to beam until we reached the top. Once there we prepared ourselves for the exhilarating leap into space and the banks below. Perched on the edge of the roof, we felt a sudden surge of fear and excitement, a vertigo that sent our equilibrium into free fall. In a moment we were into space with limbs flailing as the white rushed up to meet us. If there is a moment in childhood when you sing for the sake of singing, when you leap for the sake of leaping, then that was the moment. It is liberation. It is joy gone rampant.

The old ballpark had its seasons. During the summer baseball reigned. It was a long-standing tradition that each community fielded its own team. This was a matter of great significance since the fortunes of the local team were directly commensurate with community pride. Teams were comprised of an assortment of locals, from college students home for the summer, to the old mainstays, men who had set roots in the town, and young men between high school graduation and their first foray into higher education at college.

It was also common practice to import "outside talent" for a competitive edge. Outside talent usually came in the form of a young man with a very strong arm to be utilized on the pitcher's mound. That talent might be recruited from a location away from the competing communities so as to defuse charges of "talent raiding" among the competitors. It was also customary to arrange summer employment for the recruit. Such arrangements provided financial inducement for the recruit while keeping intact his amateur status. Direct compensation was a violation of the amateur code of ethics founded on the honor system.

It was not unknown for the parish priest to set aside his robes on Sunday afternoons for the more secular pursuits of the great American pastime and lend his talents to the local team. One such figure was Father Matthew Fettig who was assigned to the local parish. In addition to his spiritual duties, the pastor sometimes assumed the role of mentor taking over the reigns of the little league or "midget team" as it was commonly referred to at the time. Father Matthew, by some accounts, bore a well-cultivated resemblance to the popular crooner of his day, Bing Crosby. The ever-present pipe dangling from his mouth beneath a hard straw hat trimmed in gold was complemented by the customary black slacks and light

summer shirt. At social occasions Father Matthew demonstrated an insouciant charm that ingratiated him into the confidence and good graces of his parishioners. The overall effect was an elegant sophistication and social ease that served him well in the administration of his duties in the parish. Like his renowned alter ego, nature had also blessed him with a rich, deep-throated baritone voice. Encountering him on a snowy December day, you might have expected him to burst

Father Matthew, 1948

forth with his own rendition of "White Christmas."

On game day the opposition sometimes found Father Matthew's managerial style a bit enigmatic. From his vantage point behind third base, Father Matthew engaged in a series of elaborate motions designed to deceive and confuse the opposition while directing base runners and batters in the usual strategies of the hit and run, the bunt or the steal sign. Such rituals, a fundamental part of the game, assumed many variations. Father Matthew's were a bit unorthodox. From his familiar crouch along the third base line, Father Matthew dipped into the left pocket of his shirt, deftly fetched a handful of sunflower seeds, popped them into his mouth, and then cracked them open. At that precise moment, a runner on first base streaked for second. If the opposition failed to crack the code, their frustration might have been attributable to two explanations. Either Father Matthew was bestowing some sort of benediction on the proceedings, or he was invoking Divine Providence to aid the fortunes of his team.

The assistance of Divine Providence was at times much in demand. Our second baseman, not renowned for his fleetness of foot when called upon to steal a base, seemed more preoccupied with a sense of self-preservation than with the good fortunes of his team. At such times, his instinct for self-survival simply overwhelmed his competitive spirit. Somewhere between first and second base he threw up his hands flailing in desperation to cover his head to fend off the catcher's throw streaking from behind home plate. To the dismay and amusement of his teammates, he stumbled toward second base like a lumbering ox on his way to the slaughterhouse. While he seldom reached second base ahead of the ball, his cranium remained intact for the duration of his playing days. Perhaps it was an oversight that such manly feats were not immortalized in the form of a plaque bearing the image of a runner breaking for second base with his hands shielding his head and an inscription reading, "Divine Providence assists those who assist themselves."

The maxim that only mad dogs and Englishmen go out in the noonday sun is not inclusive enough. So do little league baseball players. Our practices were conducted in the middle of blazing summer afternoons. Since we did not have the benefit of sophisticated sun block lotions, we simply sweated it out. A prelude to our practices was a friendly competition known as the "grandstand climb." The grandstand climb provided a formidable challenge guaranteed to get the glands pumping. A thick wire mesh anchored to a wooden base ran from the bottom of the grandstand to its top. The object of the competition was to see who could scale the wire façade to its highest point. In order to do so, competitors approached the façade with a headlong sprint and then at the precise moment hurled themselves onto the mesh to begin the ascent. In one continuous burst of motion and energy, they dug their spiked shoes, with sparks flying, into the wire and clawed their way toward the top with a force strong enough to send a ripple of waves across the mesh. Once they had gotten as far as they could go, they began their descent in a deliberate backwards motion like a man descending a ladder. Back on the ground they inhaled great gulps of air and felt the sting of perspiration seep into their eyes. The wire mesh had left deep purple indentations and an insistent throbbing in their hands.

Part of practice was aimed at a drill designed to hone the catching skills of the outfielders. While we settled in the far reaches of center field, Father Matthew launched a barrage of fly balls into the heavens. This was done with a fungo bat, a specially designed elongated club shaped to propel the ball upwards. Ascending rapidly into a high arc, the balls seemed to hang motionless like tiny white dots in the sky and then began to plummet like rockets into the leather webbing of our gloves. We called them "dependers" because in our imaginary scenarios the outcome of the game depended on whether we made the catch at the crucial moment. Such a challenge appealed to our inventiveness. Some of us emulated the great Willie Mays and his basket catch tucking the glove to our midriff to catch the ball at the waist and then firing it toward the infield. The more fearless of us attempted the basket catch in reverse by turning our backs to the ball and tucking the glove at the base of the spine. The result was often painful when we miscalculated the ball's trajectory and felt the lancing impact of the ball against our spines. We sometimes varied our style with the under-the-leg maneuver. We executed it by resting our weight on one foot, raising the other leg into an inverted V and attempting to catch the ball with the glove under the V. From a distance our antics and the muted pop of the balls into leather seemed like a pantomime of grace and, at times, clumsy ineptitude.

Games for the adult teams were reserved for Sunday afternoons when the local ballpark became the focus of community pride and pregame preparation. While the opposing teams took their turns in the batting cages, some of us waited for the errant foul balls that came looping over the grandstand into the deep grass. Each ball carried a fifty-cent bounty for its return to the playing field. At times some of us chose sentiment over profit. Some of those balls found a place on our shelves at home alongside the treasured memorabilia of Tops baseball cards.

Other pregame preparation took place at the concession stand. Ravenous fans, in keeping with tradition, demanded the kind of cuisine synonymous with the great American pastime. That demand was met by the concession stand. Ours, painted in a muted dark green, was built on the back side at the base of the grandstand. A sliding wooden panel barred from the inside was loosened to accommodate the customers. Though the stand's subdued exterior appeared a bit drab, its contents compensated for it. Inside was a larder groaning with a rich assortment of candies, soft drinks and boiled hotdogs tucked into buns dripping bright yellow mustard down the side. On the shelves, rows of Baby Ruth, Butterfinger and Snickers bars stacked up against each other to offer the kind of sticky sweetness that lodged like mortar in your teeth. To accommodate the thirsty, a steel tub of ice water held bobbing bottles of soft drinks. Of these, only the Nehi brand lorded its superiority over its rivals, whose offerings were but a mere token of competition. Its ruby-red strawberry soda inside the familiar rippled glass bottle burst into your throat with a potency that shocked your taste buds into a sensory rush of flavor rich enough to savor again and again, its aftertaste like a long sweet goodbye. It was like a first love. It held a special affection that no rival could ever match again.

As game time drew near, rows of automobiles in single file inched their way up the gravel road toward the gate. From there they formed into rows along the first base and third base lines, which gave them a vantage point directly behind the dugouts of the opposing teams. Wooden posts with wire screens ran from the main grandstand down both baselines to protect vulnerable windshields from foul balls and errant throws. Such proximity to the action gave hecklers easy access to cast their barbs at opposing teams.

However, the true "artists of invective" seemed to gather in the main grandstand directly behind home plate. Such proximity made an easy path to the sensitive ears of the umpire. Umpire baiting, as integral to the game as the American hotdog, assumed a ritualistic distinctiveness of its own. Local fans had a special affinity for the salted sunflower seeds sold at the concession stand. The seeds, which had to be cracked open inside the mouth to extract the kernel, came in small paper packets that tore open at the corners. A novice in the art of sunflower-seed eating found it to be a formidable challenge. The older generation, however, had honed the skill to perfection. With a staccato-like precision and speed the shells shot from their mouths into small piles around their feet while the epithets they hurled like spears found their mark in the umpire's hide. Their insults often formed a strange hybrid of local German dialect and English. Thus "Kill the umpire" translated into "Dawd schalgen (beat to death) the umpire" or "Mach hea (make dead) the umpire."

Other colorful epithets became part of the repertoire as the game progressed and the piles of seeds grew higher.

Each game has its own dynamic, its own character and its own drama. Our house was close enough to the ballpark so that we could hear those sudden outbursts of drama when the home team scored a run, hit a homer or made a special play in the field. Those outbursts came in a sudden cacophony of blaring horns, raised voices and the thundering of feet pounding in unison on the grandstand bleachers. At such moments a quickening in the blood sent me racing to the scene of the drama unfolding in the ballpark.

On one such occasion I witnessed an event unique in the annals of local legend. The home team was engaged in a stalemated struggle in the late innings of the game and threatening to score with men on base. As good fortune would have it, our mightiest slugger was due at the plate. Would it be another "Casey at the Bat," or would the locals tip a brew in tribute to a great victory in the taverns that night? The opposition adhered to conventional baseball wisdom and began to deliver the pitch outside of the strike zone to walk the batter intentionally. What happened next became the topic of discussion in the taverns for years thereafter. Our version of Casey stepped forward and delivered a whack that shot the ball toward the heavens in left field. Stunned silence and disbelief soon broke into pandemonium. This time Casey had not struck out! I cannot attest to it as a fact, but I would wager that many a glass was raised in tribute that night in Mattern's Blue Room.

Maybe that home run was the last call to glory for the old park. Maybe small town teams disbanded with the advent of television, easy access to automobiles, and an evolving pop culture that offered too many affordable distractions. The old ballpark fell into disrepair. Weeds choked off the infield. Holes and rocks pockmarked the outfield. Rain washed away the chalk baselines almost overnight. The old grandstand in my hometown was razed years ago. Still, sometimes on a warm summer night or on a hot Sunday afternoon, I feel a sudden urge to stop behind where third base used to be. Maybe if I look hard enough, I'll see Father Matthew dig into his pocket just one more time to give the steal sign.

Echoes of Summer

A venerable sage once observed that when children pass to adulthood they should always retain something childlike, for life has a way of inuring us to its most simple joys. In the 1940s in the rural community of Strasburg, North Dakota, we found those joys on summer days long after April's sun had loosened winter's grip so reluctant to yield its hoard of cold. On such days we occupied the hours in the kind of spontaneous play that seems foreign to a current generation of children shackled to a technology of video games and the Internet.

For young boys, cowboys like Gene Autry, Roy Rogers and Randolph Scott, intrepid heroes of the cinema, became the stuff of our fanciful adventures. Indeed, the relative physical prowess of Gene and Roy often ignited passionate debate among us over which of them could "give it" to the other in a match of fisticuffs. Whatever the case, our adventures needed the appropriate trappings. That meant a trip to Keller's Hardware, a storehouse of treasure to rival the wealth of King Solomon's Mines. For there, I could choose among a glittering array of cap guns like the Texas Jr., the Texas Sr. and the Gene Autry. Intricate scroll-like designs above the white handles of the Texas Jr. and Sr. gave them an artificial flamboyance not as much to my liking as the unpretentious Gene Autry model with the bright orange handle and heavy steel barrel. Today's lightweight plastic/alloy models, fit for only the tenderfoot, would never have been holstered on the hip of any self-respecting cowboy. Such a breach of etiquette could only be perpetrated by a greenhorn and met with snorts of contemptuous derision from "real cowboys." Nor did I prefer the six shot rotating-cylinder cap gun so conspicuously brandished in the hands of Archie Van Beek. A six shooter may provide verisimilitude, but whoever counts the shots in a fantasy? Did anyone ever see Gene or Roy run short of ammunition? Maybe bad math and cowboy longevity go hand in hand. I preferred the functional to the aesthetic, too. After all, not once did I see one of those fancy guns in an outlaw's hand find its mark before Gene "plugged-em dead" on the draw. Maybe there was a simple moral to it. Functional beats flamboyant. Ask any bad guy on boot hill.

Our cowboy games found their perfect setting just a block from my house. There, Bobby Wickenheiser and I let our imaginations segue into turning the Wickenheiser garage into an outlaw's hideout. The concrete floor in the garage had an acoustical advantage, too. It made the pops from our cap guns ring out in sharp report stinging our sensitive eardrums like the prick of a needle. The woodpile in the upper half of the garage, a converted barn with a hay chute, became the place from which we had to ferret out the bad guys, who, in an attempt to escape the claims of justice, bolted for the chute. That's when we, demonstrating the agility of a Randolph Scott, bounded after them down the chute, overpowered them and led them off to jail. Our resourcefulness was put to the test when we converted a dilapidated chicken coop adjacent to the garage into the Coroner Creek Jail, its namesake one of Randolph Scott's westerns. A rusty wire gate over an opening in the chicken coop became bars from behind which no outlaw dared venture. *Coroner Creek*, among a long list of Randolph Scott grade B westerns, has ridden off into the sunset of cinema oblivion, but I like to think our jail paid it and Randolph Scott an enduring homage one last time.

Our summers were not wholly consumed by cowboy fantasies. If there is a common notion that slingshots and boys were part of a Norman Rockwell America half a century ago, that notion was corroborated by a common practice among boys in my hometown. We made slingshots. And we hunted birds with them. We sawed Y-shaped crutches from trees, stripped the bark, carved grooves into the crutches near the top on each side of the Y, and then tied strips of rubber from discarded inner tubes to the tops of the crutches. Leather tongues ripped from old shoes were affixed to one end of the rubber strip and tied with string in holes punched into the leather tongue on both sides. The tongues held the rocks we sent indiscriminately in swift trajectory at whatever targets we had recklessly selected. The male rite of passage by hunting, too often the brutal transition to manhood, sent young boys on journeys in search of the glory of the first kill. Mine came the day the rock from my slingshot found a sparrow high in a tree beside our house. The soft thud I heard on the grass quickened my pulse as I approached my prey. A mounting euphoria left me lightheaded. The sparrow looked small, its beak open in a rictus of death. A crimson circle of blood blotted its breast. Had the first kill been heroic or cruel? Only a hunter would presume to define "the hunter's high," but I could only feel the ambiguity of revulsion and thrill. It would be years later before I would comprehend the remorse of my deed. In retrospect, however, I think children can be forgiven for the violent impulses of their innocent savagery.

As in all towns, the hub of children's play was the playground. Ours was between two schools a short distance from our house. Plows shaped the area into a skating rink for the winter, but during summer months the playground, and especially the merry-go-round on its edge, drew children from the neighborhood. Our merry-go-round was designed for function, not aesthetics. It had no elaborately and intricately carved wooden horses, the kind seen only when the carnival came to town. No calliope ever sent bursts of musical notes into the summer night as if to spur wooden horses into a frenzied gallop. Our merry-go-round was erected with a steel post anchored at its center. Steel rods ran from the top of the post and sloped down into handrails for support to form a cone-like shape. Riders stood on wooden planks bordered by steel supports. There were no seats. Riders stood on board in a circle and then, arms pulling and legs flexing in synchronized unity, pumped the merry-go-round into motion, each turn gathering greater momentum until the force spun into a vortex of arms and legs. Steel supports on the planks, colliding with the center post, shot sparks like fireflies winking in the night while the clang of steel on steel rang out the joy of children at play.

The culmination of a child's summer often arrives with the Fourth of July. That grand event was marked by certain preliminaries. Fireworks stands sprouted on the edge of town. Local gas stations stocked the much-in-demand Zebra brand of firecrackers, so much a premium that enterprising lads hoarded supplies to sell at inflated prices when the supply fell short of demand. Zebras came wrapped in packs of thin paper that crinkled when you ran your fingers over the rounded contours of the firecrackers inside. It was the kind of preliminary thrill a boy feels even before he ignites the first firecracker. Some of those firecrackers found their way into anthills that served as imaginary bunkers in John Wayne movies. Our backyard became a World War II battleground of dust clouds and the smell of exploded powder. Firecrackers also served to create the "machine-gun-effect," a rat-a-tat of pops when firecrackers were lit to go off in rapid-fire succession. The effect reached a crescendo on the Fourth of July, but still seemed to linger days after the last Roman candle had flared into darkness.

Fourth-of-July activities commenced with the traditional parade on Main Street, where local merchants put on their best aesthetic face in the form of floats festooned in ribbons, crepe paper and trinkets of all sorts strung like sausages on automobiles, fire trucks and farm machinery. It was a special day, too, for my Uncle Joe's beige and turquoise two-tone ford. Maybe the same sort of magic that turned Cinderella's pumpkin into a coach turned the old ford into the pride of Kraft Brothers Store. Rolling down Main Street with bright colored ribbons fluttering like butterflies in the breeze, the ford found the kind of magic that turns the mundane into the memorable on the Fourth of July.

Local and neighboring bands strutted on Main Street, but the Case and John Deere tractors, the very machinery of our agrarian heritage, claimed their prominent place in that parade of Americana, too. Like mastodons of steel, they stood steadfast and sturdy like the James and Larry Schwabs and the Andy Hagers who owned them and have tilled the land for decades. If it is true that the family farm no longer passes from father to son, then perhaps the "progress" of corporate ownership that supersedes it, forebodes ominous prospects for the future. I like to think that some values are as enduring as the land itself.

The Fourth of July offered a variety of events and foods in keeping with local customs. Concession stands on the streets enticed the hungry with hot dogs and mustard spilling from buns and bottles of "July water," the local vernacular for soda pop. The Boy Scout concession stand on Main Street, however, boasted the finest dining of the day. There the pride of German/Russian women settled in steaming bowls of borscht, the renowned ethnic soup of homegrown beets, cabbage, carrots, green beans and dill in a beef-based broth of culinary perfection. Maybe it's a sentimental bias, but I daresay that the assorted additives that "enhance" the appeal of Campbell's Soup could never have met the exacting standards of those German/Russian artisans of the kitchen. Like food police, their taste buds would have blown the whistle. A discerning palate nails the culprit every time.

While sack races, foot races and square dances filled the day, all were but the prelude to the climactic event of the Fourth of July.

The fireworks display at the ballpark. At dusk the crowds came, the children at play and parents who maybe wanted to remember how it was when their parents had brought them. Flares lit up the sky into a sudden kaleidoscope of shapes and colors that scattered themselves into the night like shattered rainbows. Rockets boomed like the thunder in summer storms. Roman candles launched balls of fire scorching the night before fading into darkness. And then suddenly it was over.

That Fourth of July seems distant now when I go home. And it seems to have ended as suddenly as childhood. At home I wonder where the children are. I don't hear their voices on the playground. I don't see them playing in the yard. All I hear is a stillness in the afternoon. And yet I hope that maybe one of those rockets on another Fourth of July will thunder again and rouse us to recall how it used to be and how it might be again.

My thirty-one merit badges, but none for lifesaving

The Last Merit Badge

There is nothing more indigenous to our American character than the tradition of scouting. If the cliché, "as American as apple pie," has entered the lexicon of our native tongue, then so has "Be Prepared," the motto of every young boy who ever donned the khaki uniform of the Boy Scout. The Boy Scouts and Cub Scouts in my hometown of Strasburg, North Dakota, became part of that great scouting heritage during the 1940s and 1950s. For me, scouting became a progression, a rite of passage. It was like the minor league baseball player honing his skills on his way to the majors and hoping that his membership in the fraternity of the big leagues would not someday be revoked for want of authentic credentials.

Cub scouting offered camaraderie and new challenges. The camaraderie came at weekly den meetings, whose lure had as much to do with the comforts of the cupboard put out by doting den mothers as the challenge that scouting had to offer. No gathering ever went without the ravenous consumption of hot-buttered popcorn, homemade pie or cookies, and soda pop or lemonade. Our scouting skills might have been suspect, but no one ever questioned our talent for making food disappear like half-starved Houdinis. Ours was a "legerdemain of the palate" worthy of a Boy Scout merit badge.

My scouting skills were put to the test the first time I tried to make a kite. I labored under a severe disadvantage, however. A prevailing cultural bias at the time proscribed the use of the left hand to execute the basic motor functions. Lefthander was a designation and a stigma that connoted the unnatural and the defective. My natural inclination to execute those functions with my left hand was "corrected" by the misguided solicitude of my parents, who "rewired" me to function from the right side. The negative effects on my coordination are open to speculation, but I suspect that the dubious distinction I bear for having failed typing in high school is directly attributable to that "course correction."

Maybe that accounts, too, for the trepidation with which I approached kite-making. Diffident fingers gathered the materials. String, paper cut in the shape of a diamond, glue, and two sticks formed to make a cross over which the paper from my father's store would be folded and glued. Ridges cut into the sticks held the string that ran along the outer edges of the kite to give it a diamond shape. For ballast, a tail fashioned of rags strung together was attached to the bottom of the kite like an earth-bound comet eager to take flight.

I approached flight day with skittish anticipation and an ominous apprehension. Would my comet soar to the heavens or plummet to earth like the Hindenburg? On the playground adjacent to our house, I took the kite in hand, began to let out the string and bolted across the playground while the kite and my hopes began to rise. For a while. Then a calamity, which remains inscrutable to this day, struck a lightning bolt to my hopes. As the kite began its ascent, it inexplicably veered into the telephone wires strung across the playground. What might have been a trivial incident in the grand scheme of life took on the magnitude of cosmic catastrophe to my innocent aspirations. A tangle of string and shredded paper hung from the wires like a wounded bird. Such an affront to my naïve sense of justice and fair play demanded an explanation. None was forthcoming. Had the "gods," whoever or whatever they were, carried out a vendetta? When dismay turned to anger, I vented my rage the only way I knew. I took the name of the Lord in vain. Repeatedly, in big, bold letters savagely struck into the dirt across the playground. It was a futile catharsis. For months afterwards, the remains of my kite in the wires taunted me with malicious glee whenever I approached the playground.

My transition to Boy Scout arrived several years later, but a great scouting tradition had already taken root in Father Florian Fairbanks, who founded the first Boy Scout troop in Strasburg. Scouting in Strasburg reached its apex of glory under the guiding hand of Scoutmaster George Hanrahan when the governor of North

Dakota came to town and in a special Court of Honor pinned Eagle Badges on eight of our boys. It was a milestone. And an inspiration. It may have been the first time I knew that I wanted to become part of that elite fraternity. Maybe that Eagle Badge would adorn my chest someday. Before then, I'd have to earn merit badges. Lots of them.

In the meantime, however, my participation in boy scouting would be a vicarious one. Age specifications still excluded me from becoming a Boy Scout. I had not yet reached the minimum age of eleven. Then good fortune made a benevolent gesture. It bestowed on me the opportunity to serve an unofficial apprenticeship of sorts. My father's membership on the Boy Scout Board brought with it special considerations. One of them allowed me to join the scouts at summer camp.

Sales at the concession stand on Main Street each Fourth of July provided the funding for the annual summer camp. Our motto, "Be Prepared," found its practical application in our collective effort to meet the entrepreneurial challenge. Planks and two-by-fours from the local lumberyard were sawed, nailed and transformed into a concession stand overnight. The menu offered the traditional holiday fare of burgers and hotdogs; and when a customer requested a bottle of "July water," a vernacular term for soda pop, we fetched one of the bottles of Nehi pop bobbing enticingly in a huge steel tub of ice water. Nothing, however, pleased the palate like the pride of the local housewives' kitchens. It was the traditional German/Russian vegetable soup, borscht. Its organic, homegrown carrots, beets, cabbage and green beans were a culinary perfection no can of Campbell's soup could ever hope to rival. Supping on soup at the Boy Scout stand was as good as it got.

By the time my first summer camp with the scouts arrived,

Father Matthew Fettig had assumed the duties of Scoutmaster. He was an ebullient, energizing force sometimes given expression in a nervous, staccato-like laughter that spilled out in all directions while on other occasions, his demeanor assumed an easy aplomb seemingly unruffled by life's stresses and trials. Out of his clerical garb, his attire was that of a man at ease in light sporty shirts, summer slacks, a sporty straw hat and an ever-present pipe in his mouth. His imposing energy and insouciant manner made for an ingratiating charm perfectly suited to his duties as Scoutmaster.

Stone Lodge at Camp Richmond near Aberdeen, South Dakota

My first foray into camping came at Camp Richmond several miles west of Aberdeen, South Dakota. An imposing stone lodge in the center of the grounds served functional purposes. Inside, rows of long dining tables accommodated diners while a spacious kitchen stood off on the far end. There, some of the Boy Scouts' mothers volunteered their expertise in the kitchen by turning out hamburger steaks and goulash far more palatable than any "culinary experiments" customarily found in a tin tray over a campfire. Boy

Scout founder Sir Robert Baden-Powell might have considered it a breach of self-reliance, but I daresay that the meals turned out by the mothers were consumed with nary a twinge of conscience. Self-reliance builds character. You just don't want to do it at the expense of your taste buds.

Bunk beds upstairs gave me a vantage point from where I witnessed the resourcefulness of the scouts in their nightly entertainments. After meals the troop gathered in the dining hall to conduct a kangaroo court. Those proceedings were conducted with a mock solemnity befitting a high court. The crimes of the accused were petty, of course. The miscreant might be charged with leaving a morsel of food on his plate or leaving an unmade bed in his cabin. A jury comprised of cooks weighed the evidence sworn to by witnesses who took an oath of "Scout's Honor" to verify their testimony. The accused was often the victim of a frame-up. Allegations made by witnesses in prior collusion sealed the verdict against the victim, who was sentenced to a day of KP or to cleaning chores in the cabins. All of it was conducted in the spirit of good fellowship, the convicted often regarding his trial as a badge of honor. It was the sort of bonding that makes a robust esprit de corps among the troops.

A more intriguing recreation involved a bit of sham mysticism. After the scouts formed a circle, one of them was asked to step forward, get on his knees, raise his hands overhead and then begin to chant "a mystical native American incantation" that would reveal to him a great truth. With bewilderment and great earnestness he began his sing-song chant in broken "syllables," "Oh-wha-ta-goo-se-i-am " while lowering his upper body in synchronized motion with each syllable. He was to repeat the mantra at an accelerated speed until the moment of enlightenment when the message would be revealed to him. The message was immediately decipherable to the more perceptive, who cajoled and encouraged the chanter toward enlightenment. Those who "got it" passed on the answer in confidence and were replaced by another scout. With increased acceleration the message became apparent, "Oh, what a goose I am." Were I pressed to make an observation about it, perhaps I would say that sometimes mysticism is very mundane.

Not all of my adventures were vicarious ones. At the lake I acquired a skill integrated into a regimen of physical fitness I maintain to this day. I learned to swim. Under the patient mentoring of the older boys, my awkward thrashing in the water soon took on the proficiency of a competent swimmer. The swimming and lifesaving merit badges were a prerequisite for the rank of Eagle Scout. When camp ended at Richmond, my apprenticeship closed with it. It was time to move on and enter the fraternity of Boy Scouts.

My admission into the Boy Scouts came with a new Scoutmaster and a new uniform. Father Claude Seeberger inherited the mantle of Scoutmaster. He conducted his affairs in a modest, unassuming manner quietly efficient in an understated way. On my khaki uniform the numeric designation, Troop 74, emblazoned in white numerals against a bright red patch, stood out in conspicuous relief. The troop was subdivided into patrols. Ours was identified by the emblematic figure of a sleek, black panther sewn onto a patch on the uniform. The creature, rendered so lifelike, seemed almost real enough to pounce from the imaginary confines of its patch at any intruder foolhardy enough to cross its path. A neckerchief of yellow and blue fit around the neck. To my unsophisticated eye the uniform was an ensemble of fashionable panache.

Under the stewardship of Father Claude, my pursuit of merit

badges progressed rapidly though not without misfortune. One occurred on Halloween. The pup tent we had previously erected for an overnight camping trip at a nearby grove was found disassembled. Its tattered canvas hung from the trees like a macabre Halloween ornament. Was it the handiwork of Halloween pranksters or something else? I was never sure whether it was coincidence or curse, but in my mind's eye I saw once again the familiar image of a mangled kite dangling from the telephone wires.

Merit badges earned in outdoor skills brought new opportunities for advancement. Such an opportunity came when Troop 74 took on the challenge of building a raft in Rice Lake nine miles south of Strasburg. The planks and scrap lumber we scrounged from the local lumberyard made a platform hammered into place on the trunks of dead trees we had chopped down in the knee-high shallows of Rice Lake. The sturdy raft held nine scouts on board. I regarded such a feat as the embodiment of the scouting spirit of "roughing it." I think Huck Finn would have agreed.

Only one merit badge, Lifesaving, stood between me and Eagle Scout when events unfolded with mysterious suddenness. Father Claude had just pinned the badge of Life Scout on my chest when he informed us that he was to be reassigned. The news broke over us like a thunderclap. Troop 74 was without a Scoutmaster, and no one would replace him. No other explanation was ever put forth. My mission to reach Eagle Scout had to be aborted. It was the kind of numbing calamity a more mature perspective attempts to explain. In retrospect, I've come to appreciate an irony of sorts. I've swum thousands of laps over the years. And still the merit badge for Lifesaving eludes me.

The sentiment of fond memories took me back to Camp Richmond many years later. High weeds stood like a barrier between me and the old lodge. The sturdy lock on its door would not admit trespassers. But my feelings ran much too strong to be declared off-limits. On the shore of the lake where I had learned to swim so many years before, I found a stick. With it I carved letters that said "Troop 74" deep into the sand. I hoped they'd stay a while before the lapping waves washed them away.

Van Johnson by Tony Linck/TIME & LIFE Images/Getty Images

Come Back, Van Johnson

Do you remember when going to the movies was an event? I do because I had the good fortune of growing up in a small town where the main diversion on cold winter nights was the local theater or "Show Hall" as we used to call it. That was before the advent of "TV in '53" and the descent of the entertainment conglomerates on small town tradition.

The advent of television on the plains of North Dakota seemed, at the time, like a cultural boon, and I suppose it was. However, there is an immutable law inherent in all progress. Something is lost when something is gained. There is an inevitable trade-off.

None of us suspected that we were about to lose a grand tradition and a part of an Americana that would never pass our way again. Along with television came the extinction of the small town theater. Ours was a converted dance hall next to my father's general store in Strasburg, North Dakota. My earliest recollection of it has something to do with the yellow stains we put on its walls whenever we found an egg that didn't meet the standards of our candling process. That old theater became a convenient target for the "grenades" hurled at it by those of us who had just seen Van Johnson or John Wayne obliterate an enemy bunker in *Battleground* or *Sands of Iwo Jima*. Even its hard wooden seats were makeshift and temporary, anchored to screws in wooden slats that allowed for easy removal. Its implication was lost on us at the time because we were too caught up in the din of Van Johnson's B-52 bomber raining destruction on the enemy below. My brother "Junior" tells of a legendary scene in which Van Johnson, over chow, rapturously recounts his daring exploits in the skies during a dogfight with enemy aircraft.

When progress dimmed the lights of the old theater for the last time, new ownership built a new one on the other side of Main Street. The new one had more permanence about it. Its seats were set to concrete in the floor. It also had its own identity. There is something endearing about a small town theater with Brylcream stains on its walls from all the heads that rested on them during those vintage Movietone newsreels. Maybe it wasn't aesthetic, but it had its own trademark. Sort of like fingerprints. Have you ever seen the likes of it in one of those modern multiplex theaters? They're too antiseptic to have any identity at all. You could identify at the concession stand, too. My cousin Bob honed his entrepreneurial skills at the popcorn machine reigning over his kingdom while popcorn spilled like a lava flow over the top of the popper. Last time I saw the old machine it was resting comfortably in posterity at Keller's Hardware store.

Automated projection hadn't been perfected yet either. Our fate rested in the hands of the local projectionist, whose imperfect skills sometimes left us in a state of frustrated suspense when some glitch interrupted the movie at a crucial point. Was Roy Rogers going to kiss the girl or the horse? Such catastrophes were met with rounds of feigned outrage and derision. I don't think I've ever had a similar opportunity in one of those technically infallible multiplex theaters.

One day the inevitable happened. They began to knock the walls out of the old theater. Hollywood wanted to give audiences something they couldn't get on television. Wide screens and CinemaScope. Now we could see the flaring nostrils, huge, dark ovals, of Ben Hur's white stallions thundering to victory in the Roman arena. It was glorious! For a while.

I don't remember exactly when it happened, but one day, about my sophomore year in high school, those screws set in concrete were loosened for the last time. The seats in the old theater came out for good. Maybe television's lure was just too strong. Maybe the tendrils of the entertainment conglomerates with their assembly-line theaters already had a chokehold on Smalltown, America.

NorShor Theater, Duluth, Minnesota, 1941

Still, some remnants of that independent tradition remained, for years later I was reminded of how "it used to be" when I first saw *Spartacus* at the NorShor, one of those grand, palatial movie houses in Duluth, Minnesota. Its chandeliers and towering mirrors gave it an ornate royalty foreign to the plebeian sterility of the concrete bunkers in the "modern" multiplexes with their postage-stamp sized screens.

More of that tradition remained intact for several years in St. Cloud, Minnesota's Paramount Theater, too. Its expansiveness, plush, carpeted interior and balcony rivaled the elegance of its counterpart in Duluth, but it had a macabre charm of its own. Flying bats! Somehow *Dracula* has a different impact when the theater provides its own special effects. Cherished as an architectural and cultural treasure, the Paramount still stands like a vigilant sentinel charged with the preservation of the regal elegance from another time.

The last hurrah finally arrived several years later in south Minneapolis when I attended a special marathon screening of the *Star Trek* films to honor the show's twenty-fifth anniversary. The immensity of the screen on which I had seen *The Empire Strikes Back* just a few years before was now shrunken, cut in half, to make two screens. The once imposing hull of the Starship Enterprise seemed to have emerged from dry dock inside a Cracker Jack box. The mighty Enterprise had been scaled down to fit the Lilliputians. It was the only time Captain Kirk looked smaller that I had remembered him.

Maybe I am a sentimental relic, but if I had to choose between "progress" and the vanished Americana of my youth, I would choose the latter. I think Van Johnson would, too.

Father Matthew Fettig and altar boys,
Sts. Peter and Paul's Catholic Church, 1947

An Altar Boy's Tale of a Tail

In Strasburg, North Dakota, of the 1940s, young boys shared a common heritage. It was a given, like the Yankees winning the pennant, that when you reached a certain age of about eight or nine you entered the sacred fraternity of altar boys at Sts. Peter and Paul's Catholic Church. Our group, though not bound by any formal structure or strictures, was a de facto brotherhood bonded by the common experience of serving Mass in the local parish.

Though our group was informal, admission to it did entail certain qualifications and requirements, nevertheless. One such stipulation was mandatory. Altar boys had to recite Mass prayers in Latin. It was a linguistic barrier removed a decade or two later with the advent of the English Mass. In the meantime, however, it was a challenge so daunting it might have dissuaded the less fervent from pursuing it. We met the challenge with an eager naiveté so determined that nothing could thwart us in pursuit of our goal. In earnest we began the arduous task of memorizing Latin phrases that sounded like gibberish without the accompanying English translation at hand. One such barrier, however, loomed before us like Mount Everest. It was the *Confiteor*, the lengthy prayer of penitence that struck fear into every aspiring altar boy intrepid enough to scale its summit. Despite our most valiant efforts to master the *Confiteor*, we soon found ourselves sinking in a syntactical quagmire from which only a practiced linguist could extricate himself. Confronted with what seemed to be the irresolvable, we chose between two alternatives. One was to surrender. The other was to improvise. We chose to improvise. Early into our recital of the *Confiteor*, our cadence took on a pace that accelerated with each mumbled phrase, each incantation more rapid and more unintelligible than the one before. Presumably, our deception would pass as a prayer devout enough to elevate us into a "higher plane of communication" with the Divine. In practice, our mumblings were but the subterfuge of altar boys without even the most tenuous grasp of the Latin language. I was never certain whether Father Matthew was on to our deception or whether, in the spirit of charity, he chose magnanimously to condone our "benign sacrilege."

Altar boys were assigned to serve a given number of days. If you "had week," it meant you were to be at Sts. Peter and Paul's about one half hour before services for the ensuing seven days. In the sacristy we slipped into the traditional garb, a black or red cassock that extended from the shoulders to mid-ankle and a white gossamer surplice that fell over the shoulder to the waist. The surplice was textured so finely as to leave the impression of fingers brushing over a smooth yet hard nylon surface. It was the sort of tactile sensuousness your fingers never forget. The surplice slipped over your head with a swishing sound and settled lightly onto the shoulders. I always thought it looked like the kind of flamboyant frippery of an Errol Flynn costume in *The Sea Hawk*.

In the sacristy, we filled the water and wine bottles for the offertory and then proceeded to a chore that filled me with trepidation. Someone, in front of the parishioners, had to light the candles on the high altar. What might have been a mundane task for a steady hand became a daunting challenge to hands like mine never known for their sure and precise dexterity. From behind the altar I fetched a long pole with a wick on its end. The object was to reach high to the middle of the altar and gently touch the lighted wick to the candle until it blossomed into flame. With my back to the congregation, I stood with tremulous hands in futile frustration and attempted to find my target high on the altar. Encroaching panic soon became capitulation when I fled the altar to take sanctuary in the sacristy. If humility in an altar boy is indeed a virtue, it is a virtue I inadvertently cultivated every time I tried to light the candles. By week's end I could legitimately lay claim as the humblest of them all. On the other hand, I might have claimed a certain pride in having manifested the symptoms of a new syndrome for altar boys. It never had a name, but maybe they should have called it Calamity by Candlelight Syndrome.

Once we had dispensed with the preliminaries for Mass, we waited inside the sacristy for the service to begin. The anticipated moment arrived when the priest tugged on a bell at the entry. The resounding clang in my ears and the sudden rush of my heartbeat meant we were "on." There was a mild dizziness spinning in my head, a bit of panic-induced vertigo. I didn't know what it was at the time, but years later I learned that actors called it stage fright.

I think it was right before the offertory, the offering of bread and wine for consecration, that my partner, Jimmy Bauer, broke the tension. As Father Mathew carried out the solemn deliberations, Jimmy lifted his cassock, reached into his back pocket and pulled out three furry gopher tails. With a casual disregard for the solemn proceedings at hand, Jimmy ran the tails through his fingers like the affectionate owner of a beloved pet. Maybe Huckleberry Finn never did it, but he should have. Life is better with some innocuous irreverence in it.

More irreverence was forthcoming on liturgical occasions that called for All-Servers. The designation of All-Servers was reserved for grand occasions like Christmas or Easter Sunday and Holy Week, times when every altar boy took part in the service. Palm Sunday was one of them, and the dispensing of palms to each altar boy proved too much a burden on our self-restraint. What boy's imagination can resist the temptation of transforming a palm into a sword or a spear? With our imaginary spears and swords we pricked, with the éclat of a swashbuckler, the ticklish necks of altar boys lined in front of us in rows before the altar. I don't know whether the Lord was amused, but I hope that when my time comes Saint Peter has a sense of humor at the gate.

At communion time those about to receive the host approached in single file to kneel at the communion railing. Ours was notable for its ornate magnificence and the loving craftsmanship that went into its complex design. Maybe the hands that built it left it as an homage to the glory of God. Its removal years later left an aesthetic void that has never been filled in Sts. Peter and Paul's Church. The current practice of dispensing the host to the congregation as it files by may be more expedient; but I, for one, having to choose between expediency and aesthetics, would choose the latter.

Current services have also dispensed with an instrument once part of the proceedings at communion time. At the priest's side, the altar boy carried a paten, a circular shaped gold plate with a handle. The paten held firmly under the chin of the host's recipient prevented consecrated crumbs from falling to the floor. On those occasions when a fellow altar boy knelt at the railing, I felt obliged to nudge his Adam's apple with a slight shove of the paten. While a witness might have interpreted my prank as a mild case of hazing, I prefer to attribute it to a far nobler cause. I was merely nudging a fellow altar boy onto a path of spiritual progress.

Our journey on the path of spiritual progress was, depending on your point of view, also aided by the main event of the Sunday service. It was the homily, a lengthy discourse to a penitent congregation in need of redressing its transgressions. While a short homily may have its virtues, a lengthy one does not. Far too often, the ones I heard were delivered without benefit of Mark Twain's observation that "Few sinners are saved after the first twenty minutes of a sermon." It was customary for homilies to run a full hour. Had those sermons been more "virtuous," I daresay the departed souls from Sts. Peter and Paul's might have found their way to Heaven in greater numbers.

If some of those homilies were distinguished by their inordinate length, others were remarkable for their portentous tone. Some of Father Matthew's predecessors and successors in the pulpit seemed to have been taught in the Jonathan Edwards school of discourse. Their sermons descended on the faithful with a fulminating admonition that unless spiritual amends were made, the afterlife would be a blistering place, indeed. Those versed in early American literature might have assumed that the text of the homily was a paraphrasing of Jonathan Edwards's *Sinners in the Hands of an Angry God*. Dire admonitions resounded from the pulpit with such force I might have fancied a slight trembling in the chandeliers overhead. But I was certain of one thing. The trembling in my soul was real. The spirit of Jonathan Edwards seems to have vanished from modern worship in the churches I attend. I prefer to believe that contemporary spirits are more schooled in the virtues of mercy and forgiveness.

In addition to daytime services, altar boys were occasionally assigned to serve at Saturday night devotions in the summer. On hot summer nights, boys have more pressing priorities. They prefer to be somewhere else. Like at the movies. Though Saturday devotions ran but an hour, for me, that hour defined a familiar concept. Time is relative. An hour of rosary and confessions, though edifying for its participants, seemed not to end for a young boy with visions of Roy Rogers and his horse Trigger disposing of Black Bart at the local theater. It always seemed unfair that Roy's heroics on the screen flashed by swift as a bullet while that hour of devotions seemed closer to my idea of the eternal. I always thought those more concerned with their eternal rewards during devotions were missing too much fun. My rewards were more temporal. A young boy always thinks cowboys are more fun than prayers. That is why I bolted for the theater the moment I stuffed my cassock and surplice into the closet after church.

Summer had other rewards, too. That was when Father Matthew demonstrated his gratitude for our services. Our first reward was a trip to Wishek and a dip in the only swimming pool between home and Bismarck. The other was a ring with a gold band and a blue/white stone with a cross in the middle. You'd never find it at Tiffany's, but it was a memento I would cherish for a long time. Almost as much as the memory of gopher tails in Jimmy Bauer's back pocket.

Third building from the right (tallest) in this
1912 photo became the Kraft Brothers Store.

Before the Mall

Before the conglomerate mall and the super highway garroted the
small town economy in rural America, there stood a structure
common to the small towns of the Midwest. It was the general store,
the hub of commerce and a magnet for social events on Saturday
nights. My father Pius and his brother, Joseph Kraft, owned one
in Strasburg, North Dakota. It stood on Main Street for well over
half a century until declining health forced Kraft Brothers to close
its doors in 1970. Facing Main Street, the store's front rose upward,
the midsection, the highest point, flanked by two lower sections at
right angles. Huge windows inside the store gave visual access to a
parade of customers going about their affairs on Main Street.

The general store offered a generous abundance of goods, a
cornucopia so weighted with fresh produce, dry goods, toiletries,
and sundry items that you might have expected the structure to
burst from such a storehouse of plenty.

Apples and peaches, each wrapped in lavender tissue, arrived in wooden baskets that creaked with their succulent freight and filled bins to overflowing. Apples, piled precariously high like miniature pyramids, collapsed under their weight and scattered in a rush across the wooden floor. The fruit, unadulterated by the kind of pesticides and preservatives that technological "progress" brought a generation later, was a singular delight. Tart, crisp apples crunched when you bit into them and peaches sent rivulets of juices down your chin. Nature's bounty had not yet been "improved" by the arrogance of human meddling. Though the intervening years in search of the perfect-tasting peach or apple at the supermarket have become an odyssey of futility, my taste buds have made their peace with it. They just don't grow them that way anymore.

On the floor, rows of ripe melons, their white bellies turned downward, responded with a dull thud when you tapped your fingers against them to test for ripeness. Beside them, Nehi soda, the kind that came in wooden crates with bottles that tinkled when you carried them, sported flavors of orange, strawberry, root beer and grape.

For children, only one place in the store really mattered. It was the seat of all delight, the place where a child's taste buds met joy. It was the candy counter. Stacked in crowded rows, as if in competition for precious space, popular brand names like Walnut Crush, Walnut Hill, Powerhouse, and Black Cow tumbled forth in tantalizing temptation. One bar, however, stood apart from the rest. It was the redoubtable Seven Up. This dark chocolate confection of seven parts was a combination of caramel, cream, nuts, and jelly in a scrumptious harmony that no palate could ever forget. Perhaps its only rival was the Black Cow sucker, a delectable confection of hardened caramel under a coat of chocolate. Should any child have had the good fortune to get one "irremovably" stuck to his tongue, I daresay he might never have lodged a complaint. On some occasions a child not yet versed in life's economic realities, offered a nickel for one of the dime candy bars. At such times my father "closed the deal" by sending the child home with the ten cent Seven Up or Mars Bar joyfully clutched in his hands. Maybe it's the sort of innocent memory a child takes into adulthood. If so, my father knew that sometimes operating at a loss may be more profitable in other ways.

The candy counter also offered another enticement, the kind that seems a prerequisite rite to a young boy en route to manhood. It was my introduction to nicotine. Adjacent to the candy, on a pack of cigarettes, the flamboyant figure of a cavalier in the frippery of a Seventeenth Century nobleman brandishing a saber, lured me into the world of adulthood. His Three Musketeer-like panache was too much to resist. At opportune moments, I deftly filched packs of cigarettes and made my furtive way to the city bandstand across the street. Children weary of adult scrutiny find sanctuaries unfettered by the disapproving strictures of parental authority. Ours was under the city bandstand. It was where my friends and I bonded with booty like cigarettes to indulge in the kind of verboten pleasure exclusive to the world of adults. We didn't know it then, but the cigarette butts we left under the bandstand might have become an inadvertent homage to the spirit of Huckleberry Finn.

The general store was also renowned for its eclectic choices of meats, imported candy, and cookies that came in three-pound boxes. Chocolate-covered cookies of marshmallow and graham cracker were weighed to customer specifications on the store scale. The practiced hands of my father scooped the cookies into brown paper bags, plopped them onto the scale, and tied the bags with a precision honed by years of repetition.

Except for imported candy, the most exotic enticement in the store was halvah. This Turkish treat of crushed sesame seeds and honey wrapped in bright blue and silver paper came in eight-pound chunks. Though its presence in a rural store on the remote plains was regarded as a bit foreign, the sweet quality of its dense and oily texture quickly converted the skeptics, and halvah became a familiar favorite among the locals adventurous enough to try it. It was an acquired taste they seemed eager to acquire.

The meat counter, a smorgasbord of smoked sausage, thick slabs of bacon, and minced ham in huge tube-like casings, was my father's particular domain. There he demonstrated his expertise with the éclat of a maestro dangling morsels of sausage or ham before susceptible patrons eager to sample the wares. I was never certain whether my father's way of inveigling a customer into making a purchase by offering free samples was motivated by his generous nature or an astute sense of business. I suspect it was both and am certain that few customers left without a purchase and the savory aftertaste of smoked sausage lingering on their palates.

My father engaged his customers with an easy flamboyance, while my Uncle Joe did so with a quiet gentility equally effective. His was a soft-spoken manner, ingratiating, but not unctuous, an effortless manner of putting patrons at ease with inquiries about their well-being. His "How are you today?" seemed more a genuine concern than a mere social amenity, and should a patron inquire in kind, Uncle Joe always assured him that he was "finer than silk." It was the kind of characteristic response I still find endearing.

The miscellaneous section in the general store was a potpourri of sundry items. Ours brimmed with toiletries of all sorts. Toothpastes, liniments, band aids, grooming products, and shoe strings, that spilled over the counter edges like limp cat tails, met the daily demands of customers.

Clerk Agatha Keller and Pius Kraft
at the west wall in Kraft Brothers Store

Beside the miscellaneous section on the west wall, bolts of fabric in a selected rainbow of colors satisfied the demands of resourceful wives adept at their Singer Sewing Machines at home. Clerk Agatha Keller nimbly flipped bolts of cloth onto the counter and then, to precise specifications, snipped the fabric.

The safe in Kraft Brothers store held cash and a bit of economic history as well. After World War II an inventory of its contents bore testimony to hard times. Unpaid customer bills of over $50,000 still remained. Maybe my father and Uncle Joe, tempered by the travail of the depression years, felt a special kinship for the poor. In lieu of cash, destitute patrons salvaged their dignity by bartering chickens, sausages, eggs and even pianos to satisfy their debts. It is how the piano came into the Kraft family. In retrospect, the memory of my sisters playing "Heart and Soul" on that piano convinces me that we got the better of the deal.

Perhaps nothing in the store commanded as much attention as the conspicuous presence of my father's roll-top desk. That massive structure of gold-varnished wood rumbled like the sound of distant thunder when my father pushed its top back. When he did, stacks of bills, receipts, and business correspondence spilled out almost into his lap. Drawers jammed with rubber stamps, paperweights, pencils, and pens resisted his efforts to pry them open. Yet what seemed like disarray was an orderly chaos, for my father knew where it all was and where it all went. The paradox still confounds me. Perhaps it was attributable to my father's innate sense of organization that he was able to find order in such apparent confusion.

At the far end of the store, patrons could choose from stylish white dress shirts that bore the Butler Brothers tag from Minneapolis or from the more practical work overalls. Farmers often chose from the heaps of bib overalls with silver buttons. It is a bit of fashion irony that the mundane overall, once regarded as fit only for the field, was to become retro chic among young people two generations later. Maybe my father's buying trips to Minneapolis taught him more about fashion than I ever suspected.

Locals were also offered two styles of shoes, the practical and the fashionable. For their labors in the field, practical farmers chose the sturdy leather work shoes, but only the more sartorial Randcraft, its logo stamped in bold black letters on the inside heel, would do for the Saturday night dances at Mattern's Blue Room.

I am not certain whether it was peculiar to rural communities, but the general store became a haven for innocuous eccentrics who found comfort there. One of them, Casey, an elderly man of ruddy complexion and an unassuming air, seemed content to spend his days spitting sunflower seeds on the floor and engaging me in an unintelligible marathon of mumbling. In the spirit of good fellowship, I responded in kind, for it was soon apparent that I could not decipher his messages. Though those mumbled communications took on a ritualistic regularity that eluded my understanding, Casey appeared to take a measure of comfort in them. Meanwhile the puddle of sunflower seeds that fell at his feet encircled him in a world removed from daily cares.

None of those eccentrics was as intriguing as Ferdinand, the bell ringer at Sts. Peter and Paul's Church. That club-footed, Quasimodo-like figure appeared at the store in a dark coat flowing almost to the floor. His shuffling gait, impeded by his clubbed feet and a hunched back, forced him to walk in a stooped manner with his hands clasped behind him, making him all the more conspicuous. As sexton of Sts. Peter and Paul's, Ferdinand rang the bells before Mass and whenever death claimed a member of the parish. It was common practice at the time that during the funeral procession to the cemetery the bell tolled once for each year of the deceased's life. Maybe that is why Ferdinand's presence always evoked in me such an unsettling sense of foreboding. Someday that bell would toll for me. On one occasion, I gathered the courage to pin a "Kick me" note to the back of his coat. It was the sort of cruel prank an ignorant child perpetrates to allay a fear he does not understand, for on subsequent occasions I saw Ferdinand and my father engage in a warm repartee known only to good friends. Maybe all Ferdinand wanted was some human engagement. For all of my fears, I never had cause to believe he intended ill fortune to befall anyone. At such times I felt a chagrined remorse that only comes with a more mature perspective.

Bell-ringer tolls the bells

Perhaps it is the sparse population in rural communities that forges a loyal bond between business proprietor and patron.

Customers' faces and names take on a familiarity less common in urban shopping centers where personalized service may be a luxury rather than an expectation. Saturday, the culmination of the week's labor, brought farmers to town and the townspeople to Main Street. Saturday nights at the store unfailingly marked the appearance of Evelyn and Edna Schwab, whose weekly visits took on an immutable reassurance that all was well with the world. Both of them comported themselves with such grace and warm regard for me that my duties as a carry-out became a privilege rather than a chore. Theirs was a gracious civility time does not tarnish.

Social occasions on Saturday nights were found at the local taverns and the dance hall, Mattern's Blue Room. In an era of more conservative social mores, wives often waited in Kraft Brothers store for their husbands to conduct their social affairs with a libation or two in the tavern. It was uncommon at the time for women to join their spouses in public drinking establishments. Current social mores would dispense with such a double standard, but I suspect that the patience of many a wife was put to a stern test before the night was over.

The evening's other social event was set at Mattern's Blue Room, the dance hall adjacent to the store. The site of dances for young people and weddings, the Blue Room stood steadfast for decades as the hub of social activity. There, revelers at wedding dances shook loose their inhibitions with an abandon that might have rivaled St. Vitus himself. In a synchronized stomping of their feet at the height of a polka-induced frenzy, dancers let loose with a high-pitched yelp that erupted from the throat with such unbridled gusto you feared it might rupture the vocal cords. Our vernacular definition called it "Yooksing." It carried with force enough to rouse sleepy heads in bed for blocks around. Its origin remains a mystery to me, but I always thought it sounded much like a savage form of yodeling.

Visits to my hometown in recent years have taken me back to Main Street. There the weight of time and the unforgiving elements have left what used to be Kraft Brothers store in dilapidated ruin. Fire razed the Blue Room several years ago, but the resourceful locals rebuilt it. I think if I returned on another summer Saturday night, I might fancy the sight of the Schwab girls at the store and hear the muted echoes of a high-pitched yelp in the dark.

.

Kraft Brothers Store, mid 1920s,
left to right, Ray Volk, Joseph Kraft, Pius Kraft

After the Mall

The recent razing of what was Kraft Brothers Store for half a century on Main Street in Strasburg marked the end of an era. The building on the south side of Main Street was a landmark in this small community of German Russians. Its demise takes with it a part of history worthy of preserving for posterity, for if we do not write, then future generations will not know who we were. Part of Strasburg itself was rooted in a business that served the community for almost three generations.

The original building, operated by Balzar Wald, served as an opera house for a number of years before Joseph Kraft, Ray Volk and C.J. Vanderleest bought the building from Mr. Wald and converted it into a store in 1920. In 1920 Pius Kraft bought into the partnership, replaced Mr. Vanderleest, and assumed ownership with his brother Joseph Kraft and Ray Volk, who left the partnership in 1935. Agatha Keller, who had served as clerk for many years, entered the partnership shortly after Joseph Kraft's death in 1960, and Kraft Brothers Store then became known as Kraft and Keller. The business thrived until 1970 when advancing age forced the owners into retirement.

For several years the general store offered hardware, dry goods and groceries along with personal items like toiletries and over-the-counter medications. When the line of hardware goods was phased out, Kraft Brothers became the general store that locals came to know for decades to come.

The store, so much a part of the Pius and Joseph Kraft families, remains dear in the memories of the Kraft children. Its ambiance still kindles fond memories. George Kraft recalls "mounting the steps and passing through the front door into a magic world of exotic and mysterious smells and colors. There was a wooden barrel of ripe black olives in brine; halvah, a delicacy of crushed sesame seeds in silver foil, fresh peaches in season, shiny glass bottles of Gold Cross ruby-colored nectar, bolts of flowery printed cloth, leathery shoes and the aroma of "Krist Kindle," candy mixed with the fragrance of balsam and fir trees. I spent much of my boyhood in this mini-world. I never grew tired of going there and never got bored. The store is part of me forever."

Sister Katherine (Frances) Kraft shares a similar fondness for the candy counter where she watched children "studying the candy counter longingly, figuring out how much all the candy cost. Candy was arranged in order of cost from penny candy to nickel to dime candy bars. Seven-up, Almond Joy, Mounds and Mars were all 10 cents and out of reach. There was gum: Doublemint, Spearmint, Juicy Fruit, Dentyne, Black Jack, and Yucatan in a yellow and pink wrapper. Next to the candy and gum were the cough drops: Smith Brothers, Vicks, and Ludens lozenges. Odors and sundry items also left a lingering memory. The smell of oiled wood floor, the neat way canned goods were arranged on the shelves, the small fruit pies the Sweetheart Bread man brought, the bolts of colored percale and the material women bought for bedding, aprons and dresses, the old adding machine with ticker-tape and large handles, the cone-shaped spools of white string with which to wrap cheese and luncheon meats. Dad was particularly adept at wrapping things with white 'store paper.' " Geraldine Kraft also had a special liking for the halvah and the Goteborg sausage. "Still my favorite cold cut."

Pius Kraft, Jr. and George still remember the old radio that rested on the shelf on the store's west side. An orange light on the dial directed them to radio favorites like *The Jack Benny Show* and *Edgar Bergen and Charlie McCarthy*, which managed to filter through the static on nights favorable to peak broadcasting conditions. That short wave radio was good enough to deliver even the most distant of sounds. George recalls the night that a maniacal Adolf Hitler rant, "Vass the Deifel," rang out onto their startled ears. In the local vernacular, "Vass the Deifel" translates into "What the devil!"

Part of the store became a haven for Bob Kraft, who warmly recalls "the back room." "That was the storage room, stacked high with pasteboard boxes of toilet paper, blankets and wooden crates of produce. Those boxes could be shoved and stacked to make little private nooks. In those nooks there could be serious talks about girls, serious sunflower-seed chewing, and hilarious anecdotes about townsfolk. Just outside was the back alley where burning refuse, before the days of garbage pick-up service, ignited our imagination. All sorts of hell and damnation could be played out. 'Here! This is Hitler's house going up in flames.' "

The back room was also the place where we carried out some of our assigned duties when helping out at the store. When fresh eggs arrived from the local farmers, we had to candle them to sort out the good ones from the bad ones. Bob still remembers what he did with some of the bad ones. "But what does one do with cracked or unacceptable eggs? Those eggs had to be flung somewhere with all those Kraft baseball-arms. The best place was the wall of the neighboring building, Mattern's Blue Room. What was a greater rush than the sound and vision of a splattering egg on stucco?" The back room also became a place for games. According to George, "This same back room was our favorite place for playing hide and seek among the stacks of cardboard boxes. Another favorite sport was teasing the cellar cats by dangling a wiener on the end of store string down the cellar steps until they gave up or got tired."

Some of us were also assigned duties apart from egg candling in the back room. Al Kraft says, "I started working at the store as soon as I was strong enough to push a broom. Later my chores mushroomed with it from sweeping the floor to filling the vinegar jars, and lugging and delivering groceries. In the winter, my job included stoking the furnace, cleaning the basement, and carrying out the furnace's ashes. As a teenager I also waited on customers and took inventory." Another of Al's chores had its own reward when he cleaned the furnace each fall and "was required to clean the area around the plenum. The plenum was cone-shaped so anything that dropped through the gate would roll down to the edge surrounding the area. Mixed in the debris, I would find oodles of coins and usually some bills. I got to keep all the money I found as it was considered my pay."

The store also had to be swept at week's end, so on Sunday mornings after Mass we went to the store. There, Sister Katherine recalls "sweeping the store using large brushes to push the pungent sweeping compound across the narrow wooden floor boards." Tom Kraft also recalls performing the same chore on Sunday nights.

Over the course of years, people and events leave their mark in a very personal way. George remembers that "Late one sultry summer afternoon while we were watching a cowboy movie in the theater across the street from the store, the screen blacked out abruptly; then the manager's voice warned us that a storm was approaching. We ran out to see a sky of wicked yellow clouds. We rushed to the store just in time. Hail stones, some the size of golf balls, came pelting down. There were two large display windows in the front. We started moving the tables and counters back. A miracle! The hail stopped. Not a crack. We thanked God."

Pius and Joseph Kraft made an effort to connect with people on a personal basis that transcended the mere "business as usual." Joseph, a courtly and gentlemanly soul, always inquired as to the well-being of customers in more than a cursory way. His "How are you today?" was more than mere etiquette. It was a sincere inquiry into the well-being of his customers. Bill Kraft recalls the idiosyncratic manner in which Uncle Joe responded when Bill asked how the day was going. "Uncle Joe would always say he 'felt finer than silk.' That puzzled me for years because I always thought he said 'finer than Syl,' who was one of the townsfolk. It was only years later I realized that he was speaking figuratively. That expression, for me, became Uncle Joe's signature. It is the way I will always remember him."

Pius served as a liaison for people not versed in English. Al observes that "The store was very special to many of the German-Russian immigrants because Dad was always there. People who couldn't read or write English came to Dad whenever they received a letter in English, especially if it looked like it came from a government agency. They shook in their boots when they realized it was from the government. Must have been a carry-over from the 'Old Country.' Dad read their letters, explained what they meant and answered the letters." George has similar recollections in his account. "A very touching experience happened after World War II. I saw Dad reading a letter to an old woman in her babushka. She could not read. I think she was crying. The letter was in German from a relative who had been displaced to some remote area in Russia by Stalin after the war, and it was censored so that the location of the writer could not be known. From clues in the letter, Dad thought it had come from Afghanistan. He did that for others as well."

The store also seemed to be a hub for the locals as well as transients on their way through the area. George recalls his first encounter with an African-American. "When I was five, I went to the store one day and saw an elderly black gentleman comfortably seated on the front porch. I thought he looked a lot like the man on the Uncle Ben's Rice package. Dad told me to shake his hand. So I did." Al also relates how he saw "a Black lady with two small boys, ages about four and five. She was one of those transients who hop the freight train because they can't afford the train fare. They then stop at small towns hoping to land a job with some farmer. When she came to the store, she showed me a fifty cent piece and said, 'This is all the money I have. Give me as much food as it will buy.' Dad knew those kids were hungry." The first thing Dad did was give them some food. "When the boys were through eating, Dad outfitted them with new underwear, new shirts, new pants, new socks, and shoes. Next he filled the largest bag in the store with various food items, and then handed back the lady's fifty cent piece. She was crying when she left the store. I have never forgotten that scene." Sister Katherine also remembers Pius and Joseph "putting extra treats of cookies or candy into the boxes or bags of groceries, especially for families who couldn't afford those treats."

Other transients who happened upon the scene were Native Americans, some of whom possibly arrived from Fort Yates across the river or on freight trains passing through town. George recollects the "summer that nomadic Indians appeared and set up their tepee down by the railroad tracks. They were 'dirt poor,' so Dad gave them food and also brought them home. The father had two young boys named Little Yellow Hammer and Rain in the Face." Geraldine remembers the time she tried to coax Little Yellow Hammer into the house with three Tootsie Pop suckers. "He bolted."

Of the salesmen who made the rounds in the territory, one in particular left his mark in the world of business. Harold Schafer, who went on to great fortune with his Gold Seal Company of floor wax, plied his wares at Kraft Brothers Store long before good fortune smiled upon him. George also remembers the salesman with the peculiar manner of speech. "A traveling salesman came in and engaged Dad over one of those glass counters on the west side of the store. As this salesman was making his pitch, I found myself mesmerized by his speech. I had never heard anything like it. He spoke with a heavy whistling lisp. 'I sell sssslacksss, pantsss, sshirtsss, ssocksss, and buttonsss.' His whistled S's hissed through the air. I don't know if Dad placed any orders, or if he was just as fascinated as I."

Kraft Brothers Store is gone now, and its passing leaves bitter-sweet memories for the Pius and Joseph Kraft families. Bob recalls it with fondness and a sense of loss. "Oh, to be a kid again in the back room of Kraft Brothers Store in those glory days. What is there now for kids to compare with the back room and the back alley? Video games don't cut it." Sister Katherine shares similar sentiments. "Seeing it razed tugs at my heart and memories. It supported two families. Dad and Uncle Joe were astute businessmen and knew about 'customer service' long before that became the language of sales. Dad was smart enough to know that women would not want to buy dresses or hats in the store because everyone in town would know how much they paid for those things. He also knew the store couldn't possibly buy a wide enough variety of dresses, blouses or hats. I think, too, that we were also the only store where over-the-counter medications could be purchased." To Dorothy Kraft, the store was unique. Its passing stings her heart. "There was nothing like it in the whole world. It breaks my heart that it is going away."

For George the store was a special place, too. "In its time, Kraft Brothers Store provided a complete mini-mall before malls existed. It was not just a store; it was a place to socialize and to get solid advice from men who understood their people. More than that, it stood as a tribute and a symbol. Dad and Uncle Joe were a part of those pioneers who built the town from the beginning. That store was a symbol of the spirit of those pioneers. They were descendants of those people who in the 1800s courageously left their homelands in Europe to tame the wild steppes of Russia and a hundred years later had the foresight and courage to tame and civilize the virgin soils of America. Their courage, perseverance and unshakable faith in God made this part of America a fruitful paradise. That an old building, once known as Kraft Brothers Store, would one day be no more is a part of the human story. But as it stood, even in its sad state, it was a tribute to and reminder of those men and women, our ancestors, who made our country great."

Fall

My mother Agatha and I in the potato patch, about 1949

A Harvest of Memories

Fall is the fruit of the spring at harvest time. It is a time when the labors of spring abound in rusty fields of grain, gardens of red-rowed tomatoes and trees weighted with the opulence of ripe apples and plums. In the fall of the 1940s and early 1950s in Strasburg, North Dakota, we also reaped the bounty of the potatoes we had planted in the spring. Each spring my father hired a local farmer and his horse Prince to plow the small tract of land adjacent to the convent on the north edge of town. Behind Prince, the farmer guided the plow churning up row after row of rich, black earth in furrows that became beds for the newly-planted potatoes. Prince was suited for the task with powerful hindquarters that rippled, each step a shivering tremor of muscles tossing tufts of dirt up and down the rows. As the furrows formed, we dropped the potatoes into their beds and waited for fall.

In the fall the task of digging the potatoes began. We came

101

armed with youthful enthusiasm and spades that stabbed the earth with a reckless aim that sometimes split the potatoes in half exposing their white bellies to the autumn sun. Then we loaded the potatoes into burlap sacks, piled them into a cart and tugged them home for winter storage. At home we began to unload our bounty into the root cellar. Two ventilating pipes like misplaced periscopes protruded from the cellar ceiling to the bracing air outside from where we dropped the potatoes one at a time into the pipes. Below, inside the cellar, two of us held a sack in hammock fashion tilted at an angle to make the potatoes bounce into the bin. What might have been a tedious chore took on the drama of an air raid from one of those old World War II movies. Suddenly, we were Van Johnson dropping death from the skies in *Thirty Seconds over Tokyo* as the potatoes fell onto the sack below and left choking billows of dust clouds behind.

We also put our imaginations to more practical use. That came whenever we wanted to sample my father's supply of beer kept in the cellar for cool safekeeping. Maybe it is one of life's inevitabilities that when temptation beckons, children magically discover an ingenuity and resourcefulness heretofore unknown to them. We did. Our ingenuity was put into practice when one of us outside above lowered a string through the pipe down into the cellar. Another of us in the cellar below deftly tied the string to the cap of the beer bottle and then watched the Budweiser levitate through the pipe above. We felt a certain pride at having perpetrated that Houdini-like caper whenever another bottle rose to the occasion. I suspect, however, that our smugness was a bit counterfeit. My father was much too wise to be duped by such obvious schemes. Therefore, I can only conclude that Dad magnanimously allowed us a small victory in the-never-ending battle between parental authority and the artless plots of children.

Our root cellar was a larder of harvest bounty. Its shelves sagged under the weight of jars of home-canned tomatoes, beets, pickles, wild plum and chokecherry jellies. But the delight prized above all was the sour watermelon. Those prized melons were cultivated with meticulous care and an ever vigilant eye. Melon patches were often sequestered in the country removed from the raiding parties of neighborhood boys, who regarded such precautions as a special challenge. It was not uncommon for those marauders to search out, devour and destroy any melon patch in the county. Such feats were the subject of great boasting somewhat akin to that of the plains Indians who perpetrated coups by touching their enemies in battle without themselves suffering injury. For my part, I always regarded such acts as the cowardly bravado of boys whose masculinity might someday express itself in more constructive ways.

Women schooled in the art of melon pickling went about their business with a sure hand that concocted a brine of spices before they placed the melons into barrels for the long fermentation process. When the melons were ready, I was occasionally summoned to fetch one from the barrel in the cellar. Reaching into the barrel, I felt my arm go suddenly numb. I imagined it felt like the kind of instantaneous cryogenic freeze described in science fiction, for I felt a cold that not even the most frigid hand of winter had ever gripped. Removing my arm from the barrel, I began a frantic massaging of my hand to facilitate circulation and motion in my nearly paralyzed limb and marveled that a brine so cold did not freeze the melons inside the barrel. I was not sure my painful sacrifice had been worth the price; but Father Thomas Jundt, my Aunt Christine's brother, was sure the day he stopped in to sample the melons. At first Father Thomas seemed to nibble cautiously at the melon with a reverence most often reserved for the consecrated host at communion, but his reverence soon succumbed to the savory sour of the melon. Father Thomas with the gusto of a half-starved lumberjack devoured slice after slice. I would not presume to question the biblical dictum that man does not live by bread alone. But how about sour watermelons?

In early fall, the chokecherries on the trees common in the area were ready for harvest. Burgundy clusters of ripe chokecherries so stooped the trees with their weight that any delay of the harvest meant the fruit would fall to ruin on the ground. That is when the neighborhood children struck a bargain with Mrs. Joe Bauman, whose husband owned the local theater. The small grove of chokecherry trees in Bauman's back yard needed picking. It was agreed that for every gallon of

chokecherries picked, we were to receive one free pass to the movie of our choice. In the spirit of the true entrepreneur, we ascended the trees and picked with a zealous enthusiasm. Such labors were not without some peril, however. We had to maintain our balance, fill our pails and descend safely from the uppermost reaches of the branches. It seemed to me that some perverse law of nature had decreed that the most succulent clusters of chokecherries were like the forbidden fruit in the Garden of Eden. They always seemed just beyond my reach. Displaying a prudent wisdom perhaps a bit beyond my years, I usually decided to let Adam and Eve take their chances. I was not going to take a leap of faith to that tantalizing fruit just out of reach. At such times, I recalled a trauma in those trees earlier that summer during one of our "play Tarzan" games. The object of the game was to ape the great Johnny Weissmuller's Tarzan by traversing the grove from one end to the other without touching the ground. The feat was to be accomplished by swinging from one tree limb to another. That is when one of the boys lost his grip and plummeted to the ground. It wasn't until I saw the jets of blood spurting from the hole in his neck that its horror struck me like a blow to the solar plexus. In retrospect, I recall little of what followed immediately thereafter except that the injury had not imperiled his life. I will never be certain, but maybe that trauma in the trees on that summer day became a caveat for me never to dare the fates.

Though my sister Isabel and her husband Matt Fischer were dinner guests at our table throughout the year, we anticipated their visits during harvest time with a special joy. Those journeys from Aberdeen, South Dakota, however, always elicited a certain fear in my mother. If mothers have a special "talent" born of anxiety for the welfare of their children, then my mother Agatha was especially talented. Whenever Isabel and Matt were expected for dinner, my mother anticipated their arrival by standing with her hand on her chin behind the screen door at the top of the steps and peering intently into the driveway. Maybe she was petitioning the patron saint of travelers for their safe arrival, but whatever her motives might have been, it became the sort of ritualistic pose that might have been immortalized by an artist's portrait in homage to the protective instinct of maternal love. "Mother in Prayer for a Safe Journey" would have made a perfectly appropriate title.

Sunday dinners in the fall had their own organic flavor. That is when fresh produce from our garden became the sort of culinary delight that could never be rivaled in meals made from those chemically enhanced foods from the supermarkets. Bright orange carrots, sliced cucumbers, dark burgundy beets, sweet corn with kernels like nuggets of gold and deep red tomatoes covered the table in a display of plenty to pique the appetite and garnish the occasion with the gaiety of the season. At the table, my brother-in-law Matt often engaged in his own idiosyncratic ritual. For reasons that have always confounded me, Matt seemed reluctant to join the feast. Like an astute businessman assessing the merits and pitfalls of a business venture, he surveyed the offerings on the table with scrupulous caution before deciding to partake. After much cajolery and coaxing from the rest of us, the predictable always happened. Matt shifted his chair up to the table, looked up and said, "Hey, Isabel, why don't you give me a slice of that ham, but just a small one. I'm not very hungry." Then Matt got even more predictable. Request followed request until the food on Matt's plate grew from a morsel to a mound. By meal's end, Matt had partaken with the same gusto as the rest of us.

Those Sunday dinners at home seemed like a prelude to the

main event for Sts. Peter and Paul's Parish. That was the annual church fair, a communal sharing and celebration of the harvest's bounty and a preliminary to Thanksgiving in November. The event replenished the parish coffers and became the annual tradition of spiritual and social bonding of the congregation. My sister Isabel felt a special attachment to church fairs. Indeed, I observed that Isabel's sixth sense of detecting any fair within a 100-mile radius was akin to the use of a divining rod to find water in the desert. She and I went as often as the opportunity arose.

It is a tribute to the industrious nature of the women at Sts. Peter and Paul's that an undertaking as formidable as the annual fair could be executed with near flawless efficiency and coordination. In preparation for the meals served at the fair, they gathered in the church basement kitchen days prior to the fair and began the challenging task of preparing the meals. The banging of pots and pans turned from din to determination like the humming of a bee hive in perfect harmony. Each fall that mission of unified purpose turned into a memorable success.

The first time I entered the church basement on fair day, I was overwhelmed. By the acrid sting of cigar smoke that coiled its way into my nostrils and the roaring din of the crowd! The sting in my nostrils was not altogether unpleasant. Before dinner on Sunday mornings at home, Dad smoked cigars during his weekly reading of *The Wanderer*. Thereafter, the smell of cigar smoke and Sunday dinner became a conditioned reflex. Where there was smoke, there was food. And there was plenty of food at the fair. The staple of any fair at home and the subject of passionate debate over its delectable merits was the smoked sausage so treasured by the locals. It came from meat packing plants in Linton, North Dakota, Eureka, South Dakota, and other suppliers all vying for approval from the fastidious demands of their consumers. Each supplier had his own nuanced recipe for a sausage to animate even the most jaded of palates. Its appeal has reached across several generations and state lines. Gourmands from "Back East" have been known to fly it in to Boston.

After the noon meal, we amused ourselves with diversions like the fish pond, a game in which we flung a pole over a curtain and fished out a mystery package, usually an inexpensive trinket of some sort. Since we paid but a few cents to play, we never expected to land "the big one," a prize of great value. The stakes at the horse racing game nearby weren't much higher. There, Jake Schreiner played host to our version of the Kentucky Derby. Customers placed coins on the number of a horse and then watched Jake flick a wheel on which the horses spun in a whirling circle until they halted on one of the numbers. Rapt fascination with the spinning wheel could induce vertigo, but sometimes my ears still remember the rattling click of the wheel as it ground to a stop. It was a long way from Churchill Downs, but no losing filly on that wheel ever sent anyone to the poorhouse either.

Young boys found even more simple amusements at the fair. My friend Ed Tschosik, a.k.a. "Prairie Pants," and I played hide and seek darting among a forest of limbs in the crowds. The assigning of sobriquets or nicknames in my hometown was almost common enough to be considered a cultural imperative. Ed, a farm boy raised on the North Dakota prairies, acquired his by his habit of wearing bib overalls to school, hence the designation "Prairie Pants." Which he wore with an affectionate pride! The nickname was never uttered with derisive intent. No one suspected at the time that a generation later bib overalls would become a fashion statement on college campuses, and that Prairie Pants himself had become a fashion guru ahead of his time. Our game of hide and seek, though a bit disruptive among the crowds, seldom provoked any sort of disapproval, maybe because we were granted license to shuck our inhibitions in the spirit of boys will be boys.

Many of the games were entertaining enough, but Bingo surpassed them all in popularity and in profit-making. Corn kernels or pennies served to cover the called numbers until the more sophisticated cards with colored plastic panes replaced them. If the new ones were tidier, the old ones felt more authentic. Plastic panes don't feel like a ridged copper penny sliding across the palm of your hand. Maybe I'm quibbling, but I ranked the penny "tactile superior."

We boys engaged in one other game that caused much consternation at bingo time. We perched on the window sills near the players and in anticipation of what might have been the winning call, shouted "Bingo." Such false alarms set off ripples of confusion and indignation that might have gotten us expelled from the premises by less forgiving victims. It was a justice we probably didn't deserve, but mischievous boys seldom question the quality of mercy.

The raffle at the end of the day brought the fair to a climax. Winners usually toted home a cash prize or maybe a small appliance. The only bingo prize I ever won was a small stool. I don't mind though because I can still hear the rattling click of a wheel and the impudent shouts of "Bingo" from the window sills. I've forgotten what the stool looked like.

Time stole many years before my next fair. That was when my sister Isabel waved her divining rod one last time and found a church fair in Leola, South Dakota, forty miles from Aberdeen. We didn't know it then, but our visit there became a valedictory.

Death laid a hand on Isabel's brow twelve years ago in November. Since then, my stops in Aberdeen have become infrequent, but maybe someday I'll return just in time for a fair at one of the local parishes. Somewhere I just know Isabel will want to go.

.

"Before the Game"

A Fever in the Blood

I know when it began. I know when the fever in the blood set in like an accelerated osmosis that seeped into my consciousness to take up permanent residence. It began in 1956. That is the year my father subscribed to the *Minneapolis Tribune* on the plains of North Dakota. That is the year Johnny football fever, that benevolent affliction, visited me in Strasburg, North Dakota. I did not suspect at the time that the two of us would become such fast friends that I would never want it to leave.

St. John's University in Collegeville, Minnesota, had already become something of a family tradition. An older brother and two first cousins had already matriculated to St. John's ahead of my arrival in 1959. Stories about exploits on the football field began to trickle down from my cousins and the *Minneapolis Tribune*. The era of St. John's hall-of-famer Johnny "Blood" McNally had already passed, but the roots of a great tradition had already burrowed deep into the soil in the "natural bowl."

By the time I arrived, John Gagliardi had begun to assemble a gridiron juggernaut that would dominate the MIAC for decades to come and propel him and his program to national acclaim. Three-time All-American Chuck Froehle, whose prowess on the field took on legendary proportions, reputedly threw body blocks into on-coming traffic just for practice. Such tales, of course, were told with the kind of mythological hyperbole that soon becomes legend. It is a legend that has survived and thrived throughout the decades.

The first time I entered the natural bowl I knew that I had encountered something unlike anything I had seen before. Before me lay a meticulously-groomed field of grass so verdantly lush, so pristine that any human imprint on its surface seemed almost a desecration of its natural beauty. From that field of Eden, brilliant green blazed with a piercing intensity that almost brought tears to my eyes. The field itself lay in an oval surrounded by towering trees that became murals of flaming reds, oranges, yellows and gold on bright October afternoons.

It is a pristine refuge for Division III competition, a sanctuary far removed from the world of major college athletics and professional sports soiled by academic fraud, drug abuse, prima donna narcissism, recruiting violations and an "ethic" that sacrifices the integrity of the game for a win-at-all-costs imperative. If St. John's boasts a near perfect graduation rate among its athletes, it is because learning precedes winning. At St. John's the designation student/athlete is not an oxymoron. Chances are that the Johnny quarterback will not tell you that the Thomas Wolfe Society is an animal rights advocacy group. When Blake Elliott departed in 2003, he took with him a fistful of school records. And a degree in biochemistry. Too often in the National Football League, "degree" has come to define the severity of the latest charges leveled against one of its players.

While academic standards are not compromised at St. John's, neither is the joy of the game. From the seats in Clemens Stadium, Johnny practice looks more like children frolicking on the green than the rigors of young men engaged in the discipline of athletic competition. In the exuberance of the moment, an offensive lineman rolls his 260 pounds into a ball and rumbles down the field, or a wide receiver snatches the ball from the clutches of the kicker and puts a foot to it sending it into the stands. It is the kind of spontaneity born of a love for the game, a spontaneity too often stilled by the extravagant contracts and mercenary motivation of professional sports. The only agenda at St. John's is to nurture a love of the game and to get ready for St. Thomas or Bethel. Not the National Football League or Ohio State.

More of that joy, too, is rooted in the ritual that precedes and concludes each practice. That is when Gagliardi gathers his team on the field. I have never been privy to those proceedings, but the genuine affection they seem to elicit makes for the kind of bonding that athletes take with them long after graduation. Maybe that is what accounts for the kind of loyalty that sends the sons of athlete-alumni to St. John's to play for the grand old patriarch. It is a solicitous paternalism that has endeared him to generations of alumni on and off the field. That intergenerational bond has become the rock of a tradition steeped in excellence and achievement.

That same paternalism may well account, too, for Gagliardi's ban against full contact scrimmages. The prevailing wisdom in the game of football would likely regard such an unconventional approach as near sacrilege, the strategy of a maverick coach. My initial disappointment at such a precaution soon gave way to the wisdom behind it. Gagliardi recoils from the prospect of serious injury to a player, not because it will jeopardize his prospects on the field, but because it will jeopardize a young man's future.

My personal contact with Gagliardi has been limited to coincidental encounters in the halls. On one such occasion a bemused Gagliardi, observing that the high school letter jacket I wore bore colors identical to those of Minneapolis De La Salle, inquired as to why I was not on the team's roster. Such an inquiry was flattering, but the chasm between Strasburg High School and St. John's and the MIAC was too far to bridge. The prospect of my landing a spot on the roster would have demanded a magnanimous leap of faith by Gagliardi and an even greater one from me. Such a fantasy would have been tantamount to Mr. Average making it at Notre Dame. It was a presumptuous notion I immediately dismissed. The ensuing years confirmed what I had always known.

My participation in the great tradition would remain strictly vicarious.

While the ensuing years far removed me from Clemens Stadium, they did nothing to separate me from my grand passion. The fever lay in abeyance until St. John's reached the national finals in 1965. Circumstances kept me from the game. I had obligations to the U.S. Army and was on board a ship crossing the Pacific Ocean for a tour of duty on Okinawa. The technological age of the Internet had not yet arrived leaving me isolated half a world away from St. John's and the media. And the Johnnies were up against Linfield, Oregon, for the NAIA crown. Two weeks across the Pacific Ocean on an army tub test even the sturdiest of physical constitutions, but the tsunami of sea sickness roiling in my stomach seemed less an ordeal than the suspense of waiting for the final score. That suspense ended the moment I set foot on Okinawa. There in a refuse disposal lay the military's overseas newspaper, *The Stars and Stripes*. I rifled through its pages with a frantic hope that I might find the score. And there it was. St. John's 33, Linfield 0. A non-believer would have ascribed the finding of that score to coincidence. I ascribed it to providence.

Practicality and providence brought me back to Central Minnesota in 1993. Employment opportunities and my network of friends were still intact. So was an intuitive conviction that Johnny football and I were meant to rendezvous. We met again often on game day. Over the years, upgrades at Clemens Stadium had replaced the natural grass with artificial turf and a new scoreboard. What remained constant, however, was the quickening in my blood when the team took the field. A scarlet wave of 170 Johnnies rippled down the field from north to south in an intimidating show of numbers. A surging exhilaration scrolled up the long years as if I had never left. Maybe the freshman in me will never die.

"Taking the Field"

That exhilaration was but a foreshadowing of what lay ahead in the 2003 season. In a fairy tale scenario that any Hollywood agent would have dismissed as too contrived, too improbable and too incredible, St. John's reached two milestones. The first, a win over Bethel on November 8, 2003, made Gagliardi the winningest coach in college football history. The second took them to the summit and the Holy Grail of Division III football in the national title game against a Mount Union behemoth boasting a mystique of impregnable invincibility and riding a fifty-five-game winning streak behind an offensive line almost big enough to rival the mastodons in the National Football League.

In the St. John's locker room another kind of drama was taking shape. All-American Blake Elliot was dedicating the biggest game of his career to his brother Adam in recuperation from severe injuries suffered in an auto accident. What might have been maudlin excess in a hackneyed Hollywood script turned into the poignancy of real human drama down on the field.

Near hysteria set in as I watched the miracle unfold on the field. Pacing frenetically like an expectant father, I watched St. John's dismantle Mount Union. David's rock had found its mark. Goliath was beginning to fall with a crash that would send tremors across the playing fields of Division III football.

Sports, like life, has its epiphanies, a sudden flash of truth or the realization that an elusive dream is about to come true. One came when Mike Zauhar stepped in front of a Mount Union receiver, plucked the ball from the air and bolted 100 yards down the sidelines for a St. John's touchdown. On the sidelines Blake Elliott leaped skyward in a dance of celebration while pandemonium exploded on the St. John's bench. Then Elliott, whose All-American credentials read like a resume of legendary feats, provided another one. Like an artist in a farewell appearance, Elliott closed his career with the kind of virtuoso performance that becomes myth among the alumni faithful. Near midfield early in the fourth quarter, Elliott took a hand-off, shook off a defender and sprinted fifty-one yards up the middle for a touchdown. It was a fitting homage to his brother Adam. And a measure of poetic justice. An official's error in the third quarter had nullified the game's most spectacular play. St. John's was inside the Mount Union ten yard line when Elliott turned to his repertoire of magic one more time. Loping into the end zone, Elliott extended his body, planted both feet inside the endline and cradled a pass to his chest with two defenders clinging to him in a futile attempt to knock the ball loose. The official ruling declared that Elliott 's feet had crossed the endline. Instant replay confirmed what I knew to be true. Elliott had made the catch inbounds with a panache that was the summation of his spectacular career. It is how I will always remember him. My only regret is that Norman Rockwell was not there to put it on canvas for posterity.

Convent near Sts. Peter and Paul's Church, Strasburg, North Dakota

A Frisson in the Fall

Life is a time of seasons each with its own gifts. Perhaps nature, afraid she might bore us with the monotony of endless summers and winters that induce our psyches into prolonged hibernation, feels obliged to give us respite. So follows spring and the genesis of new life. But, for me, no season so invigorates the body and imagination as the fall.

In my hometown of Strasburg, North Dakota, I always regarded August 15th as the demarcation point between summer and fall. The sun's anvil of summer heat had given way to the high still stars and the bracing cold of fall nights. Fall brought the kind of chill that quickens your step at the first tingle in your toes. In a less environmentally conscious time, it also brought the smell of burning leaves. Though I never acquired the habit of smoking, I always thought the intoxicating smell of burning leaves very much akin to a long, mellow draw on a favorite pipe.

While the change of seasons invigorated the body, its energy also roused the imagination and fanciful disposition of anyone susceptible to the bewitching season of Halloween. Perhaps it was my early acquaintance with Washington Irving's *Legend of Sleepy Hollow* or the ghost tales spun in bed late at night by my older brother George that left me so susceptible to the spirit of the season. If the ghosts of July seem docile, the spirits who come alive in a tale told on Halloween delight us with menace while they shoo away the summer spirits like mere wraiths.

In keeping with the spirit of the season, I began a ritual of nightly visits past the old convent near Sts. Peter and Paul's Church. The convent, which had once domiciled the Notre Dame nuns who staffed the faculty in our schools, seemed an architectural anomaly by daylight amid the prosaic dwellings of the town. By night it seemed more so, pervaded by an aura foreboding enough to conjure visions of Hawthorne's *House of the Seven Gables* or Poe's *The Fall of the House of Usher*. The structure, resting on a spacious lot, ran from north to south. Its entrance on the south side was approached by steps that reached to a porch-like landing with circular white columns rising to an upper level with a view toward the south. The convent, which stood at a considerable length and height, was lined with rows of windows on both sides and both levels providing a view for spirits, real or imagined, to the outside world. The overall effect was that of old-world quaintness, intriguing, but forbidding and inaccessible. Its inaccessibility became apparent on those occasions that brought me to the convent with an order of groceries from my father's store. Whether it was by edict of their religious order or by individual prerogative, the nuns at the convent, apart from their educational responsibilities, lived in seclusion. The groceries I was charged with delivering were always ordered by phone. Upon arrival at the convent, I was met cordially at the door, but never allowed beyond the "forbidden zone" of the front parlor.

During my visits to the convent grounds at night, I encountered a rather curious object, which seemed almost at once to transfix me to the spot. It was the figure of a statue holding a child, the sort of religious icon found in churches. This one, with a face formed into sharp angular features and a tuft of beard, stood before me draped in flowing robes commonly depicted on biblical figures. The eyes, sunk in the darkness of night, left no clear impression, but the benevolent smile I perceived on its face at first glance seemed to curve into a foreboding malevolence that kept me rooted to the spot. The impulse to flee was countervailed by a paralyzing fascination with the strange object before me. My heightened senses may have deceived me, of course. The incongruity of a religious icon inducing fear is an ironic contradiction, but the shudder racing up my spine was very real, indeed. It's the sort of frisson your psyche never forgets.

Behind the convent lay another site I passed, but never approached during my nightly sojourns. Speculation held that the area just adjacent to the parish cemetery was also the resting place of nuns who had been former tenants of the old convent. The wall of trees shielding the area from view, though not a physical barrier, seemed a declaration of off limits to intruders with a curious bent. I preferred to regard the cemetery as sacred and, therefore, never set a tremulous foot upon it lest I desecrate its hallowed ground.

Adjacent to the nun's cemetery and the convent stood another structure that appeared to be made of concrete or stone. It rose from the earth upward at an angle so as to give the impression of a mausoleum protruding toward the sky. Though not large in dimension, the structure seemed to thrust itself upward with such force that a fervid imagination might have regarded it as the desperate attempt of incarcerated souls to free themselves from their earthly confines. A more mundane explanation put forth by some of the locals was that the structure was a root cellar for the storage of perishable goods. The latter explanation is the more credible; but such a scene seemed more inspired by Poe's *Tomb of Ligeia*, for the labels on those jars of perishable goods might have been, for my part, more like the inscriptions on a sarcophagus. That is when fear displaced my sense of curiosity. I never entered that cellar.

The parish cemetery of Sts. Peter and Paul's lies just north, close to the old convent. The road at its entrance is a well-worn trail of furrows left by years of funeral processions. A fence encircles the area while a large gate allows admittance in the front of the cemetery. At night outside the gate, my fancy took full license as I watched moonbeams fall over skeletons in repose stirring them from their graves to alight on their tombstones. The purpose of their resurrection soon became clear when they began to dance an unbridled jig of fleshless limbs thrown askew in all directions while the clatter of bones resounded in the night. Maybe they were celebrating the emancipation from their graves, for soon the dance quickened its pace and surged to a climactic thunderclap that left only a sudden stillness in the night. Preternatural lore, according to certain sources, ordains that spirits who rise from the dead must return to their graves before daylight. Dancers of the macabre do not have time to tarry.

Dr. Phibes pounds mad chords on the organ

No setting seemed more suitable for the ambiance of the season than Sts. Peter and Paul's Church, a signpost to spiritual comfort and reassurance by day, but to sensibilities of wild imaginings, a portal to unsuspected chills at night. A stop there on my seasonal itinerary was mandatory. The church's ornate magnificence of ceiling murals, stained glass windows, glittering chandeliers and religious icons is deservedly cherished and prided by the parishioners. But no ornamentation or functional attraction surpasses the great pipe organ in the choir loft. That great instrument of heavenly chords, so long an inspiration to generations of worshippers, now seemed to serve an unearthly purpose. The spirit of those B horror movies from American International sat at the organ in the choir loft. There, Vincent Price in billowing black robes pounded out mad chords on the organ with a messianic fervor worthy of the Abominable Dr. Phibes. Discriminating tastes, of course, would have dismissed it as high camp and the clichéd gothic trappings of tawdry entertainment worthy of condescending scorn. But the tremors in my knees knew the truth. Sometimes high camp becomes high anxiety.

In the darkness, another sound more subtle than the peal of organ music pricked my ears. Creaks of protest from old tired floors met each step I took; and though my ears may have become susceptible to auditory illusion, padded kneelers in their pews, as if burdened

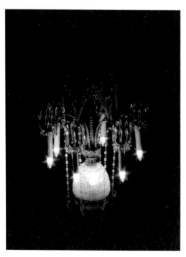

Chandelier at Sts. Peter and Paul's Church

by some unseen weight, grated against their moorings. What that unseen weight might have been, I dared not speculate. Overhead, chandeliers seemed to cast an incandescent glow against the darkness and appeared suspended, fixed without moorings, their lights like torches in the recesses of ancient catacombs.

The stained glass windows at Sts. Peter and Paul's are a panoply of saints and scenes of spiritual splendor that have edified congregations for nearly one hundred years. No image is more conspicuous and compatible with the Halloween season than the one near the confessional on the east side of the church. There, Saint Michael the Archangel stands with

Stained glass window at Sts. Peter and Paul's Church

spear in hand ready to deliver divine retribution to the demon under his foot, the silver tip of the angel's spear a lance to pierce the very heart of evil's core. Perhaps it is an oxymoron of sorts that an image symbolic of the triumph of good over evil can be at once both edifying and terrifying. It is also the image that evoked in me the trauma of a childhood nightmare from many years before. In that dream I, the penitent sinner, knelt in the confessional and began a recitation of my sins when an unsettling suspicion arose. Perhaps the list of my transgressions was falling on unhallowed ears behind the confessional curtain. Indeed, it was. Satan himself, notching another groove on his pitchfork at the prospect of adding me to his "list of the lost souls," sat grinning sardonically on the other side of the curtain. The burgundy curtains of velvet and intricate designs of scrolled gold on the confessional's exterior still haunt me with an eerie luminescence perfectly suited to the ambience of Poe's *Masque of the Red Death*. A more rational equilibrium that comes with maturity and intervening years should put such dreams to rest, but I would be dishonest if I failed to confess that I have never been able to read *The Exorcist*.

Confessional at Sts. Peter and Paul's Church

Circumstances have not allowed for visits home in many Halloweens. Some changes will have left their mark. Sts. Peter and Paul's Church will stand steadfast to serve more generations of the faithful, but years have passed since my last walk by where the old convent once stood. You will forgive me if a certain reluctance dissuades me from returning on Halloween. I fear I might find in the moonlight the figure of a cold statue with a portentous smile on its face.

Winter

Real homemade ice cream with chokecherry topping

Frozen in Time: Homemade Ice Cream

Are you old enough to remember what homemade ice cream used to taste like? I do because fifty years ago on the plains of North Dakota the making of it was a tradition common among the German-Russians who had immigrated to the Great Plains. Convenience foods, a ubiquitous staple in the modern freezer, were a luxury unknown to the industrious resourcefulness of immigrant housewives who prided themselves on "making it from scratch." The advent of the Schwan's ice cream truck was still several decades in the future.

One such housewife was my mother Agatha who, though renowned for her incomparable soups, was likewise recognized for her homemade concoction of vanilla ice cream. One of the prime ingredients for this palate pleaser, vanilla extract, came courtesy of Albert Geigle, who plied his wares with house-to-house calls in a truck proudly bearing the logo of the Watkins Company. That portable supermarket of spices soon became such a fixture in the neighborhood that it might well have served as an inspiration for one of those sentimental Norman Rockwell renderings in the *Saturday Evening Post*. I do not recall precisely, but I suspect a tacit family tradition held that at the proper time certain responsibilities were passed on in descending order from the oldest male member of the family to the youngest. The chopping of ice became one of those minor rites of passage I welcomed with an exuberant sense of purpose, for I was proud to inherit the mantle so faithfully borne by my older brothers.

Like my brothers before me, I had to take precautions against the harsh winter cold. That meant swathing myself in a pair of long johns, an undergarment fashioned to cling to the body like a second skin from shoulder to ankle. The long johns were distinguished by two features, a row of buttons down the front from shoulder to waist and a strategic flap in the rear. You entered the garment by placing your weight on one leg while slipping into it with the other and then closed the snug row of buttons down the front. At times, the maneuver proved to be precarious. Any loss of balance sent you tumbling to the floor.

Footgear came from my father's general store. The standard overshoe at the time was made of glossy rubber imbedded with a row of sturdy metal buckles that snapped firmly shut. With the addition of a cap, gloves and woolen stockings, the ensemble was completed by a sheepskin coat, a heavy garment that ran to mid-thigh with a thick woolen lining reaching to the top of a high collar stiff enough to feel like plated armor. Though its stiffness inhibited free movement, it did serve to ward off the penetrating wind. Buttoning the coat posed a challenge, too. Firmly anchored by heavy thread, the buttons stubbornly resisted any attempt to lodge them in their holes. This exerted enough pressure to bring the hands to the verge of cramping. At such times, I set aside my male pride and humbly asked for help.

If there is one constant during a North Dakota winter, it is the unrelenting winds from the northwest. Their sting grips the inside of your nose like a frigid pair of vises. The snow packs into a hard shell on the outer surface and then caves in with each footstep to leave a crunching sound beneath your feet.

Properly attired, I made my way to the source of the ice, the high school gymnasium adjacent to our house. The old gym, constructed as part of a government work program during World War II, was a massive grey building with metal drainpipes that fit together into sections that ran down the side of it. On milder days, the winter thaw streaming down the pipes solidified into chunks of ice as temperatures dipped by late afternoon.

To carry out my task, I armed myself with a burlap sack and an axe that bore the marks of many winter wars. Jagged cracks ran up and down its steel head held in place by a wooden handle splintered by years of wear. Placing myself on my knees, I let loose with a cannonade of sharp blows to the pipes and waited for the ice to rattle down the pipes into the sack. Time and again, I delivered a flurry of blows until the sack began to fill. Then, satisfied that I had enough, I slung the sack over my shoulder and trudged back to the warmth of the house.

The backroom in our house provided the usual utilitarian purposes, its concrete floor and drain put to use on washdays. I found the concrete base suitable for another purpose as I hurled the sack over my shoulder and brought it to a smashing thud against the unyielding surface of the floor. The impact shattered the ice into brittle shards then suitable to fit down the sides of the freezer when the mix was ready for churning.

In the kitchen my mother assembled the spices and ingredients. With a deftness perfected by years of practice, her hands swiftly cracked the eggs into a bowl and then added precisely measured portions of sugar, cream, milk and a potent concentration of vanilla extract. Then, with a sturdy wooden spoon, she whipped the mix into the desired texture with a vigorous concentration that sent muscles rippling from shoulder to forearm.

As my mother went about her chore, I often hovered nearby in anticipation that some distraction might divert her concentration long enough for me to yield to a delicious temptation. I had to sample the mix. At the opportune moment, with a sleight-of-hand that would have rivaled the dexterity of a magician, I darted a finger into the mix at the bottom of the bowl and then touched it to my tongue to savor the sweetness.

When the mix was ready, she poured it into a steel canister that snapped into metal grooves in the bottom of the freezer. A device of wooden slats with steel supports inside the canister then rotated the mix allowing it to harden during the freezing process. Once inside the freezer, the canister then locked into grooves in a handle at the top to facilitate the rotation process. Ice down the side of the freezer was sprinkled with coarsely ground rock salt forming a solidified mass of cold to expedite the freezing.

Then I began the chore of hand-cranking the mix. Seating myself on a stool and tilting my weight forward, I began to rotate the crank in a continuous arc that soon brought beads of perspiration to my brow. So strenuous was the challenge that I was forced from time to time to desist and replenish my stamina with a cold glass of water. The family freezer, an old bucket of wooden pieces ringed with wire, creaked in protest as I diligently went about my labor. This marathon of toil, though less than an hour in duration, soon taxed my energies to exhaustion. The rewards, however, compensated for all my efforts.

Those rewards were reserved for Sunday family gatherings. For it was then that my mother crowned her festive repasts with the kind of homemade ice cream revered by generations of grateful diners. Seated around the table, we watched huge scoops of ice cream dumped into our bowls. The dessert was topped with chokecherry jelly, a burgundy-colored confection made from the fruit tree indigenous to the area. In eager anticipation we watched ribbons of jelly stream down from the top of the scoop to settle into tiny pools at the bottom of the bowl. Those of us with fond memories of it recall the bittersweet tartness that lingered delightfully in our taste buds long after we had consumed it.

The ice cream, too, was so smoothly textured and the vanilla so potently flavorful that I have yet to find their equal in the imitation-vanilla "store-bought" varieties at my local supermarket.

I became so fond of it that on cold winter nights when the family had retired for the evening I could not resist the urge to slip into the backroom where my mother kept the canister of ice cream submerged for good keeping in ice water. Quietly I opened the canister and, with spoon in hand, began to feed directly from its contents.

My older sisters, fastidious about such minor breaches of dining etiquette, would have been offended. I, however, never one to let etiquette get in the way of my appetite, have allowed that transgression to rest quietly on my conscience.

Angels over the Rooftop

In the German-Russian community of Strasburg, North Dakota, Christmas was heralded by an annual event that every child anticipated as the official harbinger of the Christmas season. It was the arrival of Santa on Main Street. Such occasions were reserved for Saturday afternoons when children hurried downtown in eager anticipation. Somehow Santa in a sleigh always seemed like an artist's rendering on a Christmas card or part of Christmas lore so deeply embedded in our collective consciousness that its authenticity could not be impugned. Our Santa always arrived in a pickup truck. Maybe that was the first time I willingly suspended disbelief. My credulity was tested further when Santa bent to reach his bag of gifts and the very familiar face of local farmer, Henry Dosch, flashed ever so briefly from under Santa's mask. Sometimes life's illusions should remain intact, sacrosanct and inviolate. Children need them because they become a part of the joy of growing up. If a wiser hindsight inevitably divests us of our childlike illusions, I suspect it is often with a pang of regret. The bags full of peanuts and oranges that Santa gave us were real and so was the free matinee that followed at Joe Bauman's theater on Main Street. Besides, I wasn't ready to rush toward adulthood any sooner than I had to.

If Santa's arrival on Main Street meant Christmas was imminent, so did the arrival of my brother George from prep school. My brother's homecoming from St. John's Prep School in Collegeville, Minnesota, became the inspiration for a traditional prank for the many Christmases that followed. While I feigned sleep and waited for my brother's arrival in the night, the pillow I had propped above the bedroom door lay ready to welcome him home with an innocuous plop upon his head. It worked that time and times after. Of course, I was never sure, but, as the Christmases piled up and the pillows kept falling, I began to suspect that my brother had become a knowing accomplice in my prank. It became our tacit way of commemorating his coming home again.

The Christmas trees arrived at my father's general store in early December. That meant we got first dibs at the trees. They came in great bunches with their short, prickly needles and the smell of balsam so fragrant that its lingering scent, the smell of Christmas, became a permanent part of the season's trappings.

On the floor beside the tree, the Virgin Mary, Joseph and the three wise men paid homage to the Christ Child in the manger. Our tableau of miniature figures rested on soft cotton "snow" flanked on one side by a small ceramic Christmas tree embellished with colored glass cones jutting upward from the surface. The cones emitted light from within like sparkling necklaces draped around a tree of flaming ornaments of red, green, yellow and blue.

Perhaps no tradition seems more incompatible with the Christmas season than the one passed down to me orally from my parents and older siblings. It was the arrival of a creature so fearsome that his name still lives in the pantheon of mythological ogres. He came in many guises and identities during the Christmas season and is still spoken of in many cultures with awe and trepidation. This cross-cultural boogeyman was known as Ruprecht, Black Peter and other names. In our culture we knew him as the Belzanickl. Legend holds that his appearance at Christmastime was an admonition to children to mind their manners and behavior. Miscreants not "scared straight" would suffer consequences more severe than they could imagine. Good fortune precluded me from ever having encountered this ogre, but accounts of my elders and my imagination envisioned him in a sheepskin coat and high collar, which left his face obscured in shadows. In his hands he carried chains whose rattle sounded his ominous approach throughout the town. His posture was stooped forcing him to walk in a shambling gait to bear the burden on his back. On his back he carried a sack bulging with contents swirling in roiling desperation in an attempt to escape. What the contents might have been I dare not speculate, but I have often wondered how many parents conducted a head count of their children after his departure. All of this may be only embellished legend and hearsay. Or maybe the Belzanickl was the agent of fear, an accomplice in conspiracy with parents intent on correcting their children's behavior. Were I pressed on the matter, I would postulate that any reference to the Belzanickl would elicit a knowing smile from parents who felt assured that their children's deportment would be quite acceptable for the foreseeable future. Whatever the truth may be, the Belzanickl seems to have been relegated to a safe distance in myth and legend while each Christmas children celebrate the season in blessed ignorance of his passing.

The Belzanickl makes his rounds

A custom far more suitable to the season was the visitation of the angels on Christmas Eve. Their coming, anticipated with awe and wonder, brought the bestowing of gifts to the children and the singing of hymns. Appearing with a soft flutter of wings, these emissaries of grace and goodwill kept their appointed rounds in each household. Before us they stood like apparitions in diaphanous robes gathered under wings of pale blue. Behind their veils their faces glowed with the luster of fine porcelain. These heavenly creatures brought gifts of another kind, too. To accommodate an older generation not well versed in English, the angels sang the venerable "Silent Night" in English and German. I daresay that this

bilingual gift in song was cherished far more than the ephemeral and commercial trappings of the Christmas season. Not until after the hymns had begun, did I suspect that this ethereal illusion was the handiwork of the Burgad girls or the Schwab girls whose voices seemed suddenly quite familiar. It was customary at the time for young ladies, in prior arrangement with the parents, to make their rounds about the town. In keeping with the spirit of giving, a purse was passed for the deposit of gratuities, and so it was assured that heaven got its due.

Angel lore made another contribution to the celebration of the holidays. When my young niece Elaine came to visit, we took her upstairs to a vantage point from where we could see my Aunt Margaret's house across the school playground. Then, when we had diverted her glance for but an instant, we broke into feigned excitement proclaiming that angels in a celestial dance of swooping arcs had just appeared over the roof of Aunt Margaret's house. Somehow the angels always seemed to elude my niece's glance. Yet those angels were just as real as we wanted them to be.

Midnight Mass brought Christmas Eve to a climax at Sts. Peter and Paul's Church. Built in 1910 it is an imposing edifice of brick and stone. Its steeple extends upward to such a height that the devoted worshipper might well regard it as the first step toward heaven.

In rural communities the church stands not only as a repository of spiritual values, but also as a source of great pride in the community. This was especially true at Christmas when pastors and parishioners celebrated in a fashion suited to the grand occasion. Inside the church, strings of blue lights sprinkled the trees near the side altars. Chandeliers anchored to chains in the ceiling hung down the center of the main aisle to brighten it with festive gaiety. In the sacristy, altar boys who had unwrapped their gifts on Christmas Eve compared their "Christmas bounty" in an amicable competition of one-upmanship.

The ceremony began with hymns from the choir loft above the

congregation. A great pipe organ bellowing chords from the loft sent vibrations so forceful I feared the chandeliers might shake themselves loose from their moorings. Before the ceremony ended, Father Matthew Fettig, renowned for his musical gifts among the parishioners, demonstrated his virtuosity on the violin with a rendering of "Panis Angelicus." While the hymn may be common to many liturgies during the season, a violin performance of it in a setting so culturally remote is a rarity to be treasured and a memory to be preserved forever at Christmastime.

After Midnight Mass my mother served the traditional meal of ham and homemade sweet bread. The bread, braided and baked to a dark brown, was reserved for special holidays only. The ham, baked inside a doughy crust to retain the juices, became such a temptation that I would often surreptitiously slip into the root cellar, lift the roaster cover and "fetz" succulent pieces of ham. Fetz in our local vernacular was a verb describing a picking like motion with the fingers usually at something irresistibly good. Indeed, the ham was ambrosia, food for the gods. And maybe the angels, too. I still believe they fly over my Aunt Margaret's roof every Christmas Eve.

Winter Bright and Dark

It is a cliché, of course, that in retrospect we see life through the proverbial rose-colored glasses, but I see the winters in Strasburg, North Dakota, of the 1940s and early 1950s through a frosted prism of colors bright and dark. Those winters were bright with the joy of childhood games and dark with a cold that held us in a killing vise.

We played some of those games on Dosch Lake just on the east edge of town. There I wobbled on my ice skates, my stumbling attempts to maintain my balance like an arctic penguin with its flippers all askew careening across the ice. I was never quite sure whether I was breaking in my skates, or whether my skates were breaking me. Shrubs poking through the ice made the lake an obstacle course. Careless skaters who stubbed their toes on them went sprawling into a face-first free fall on ice rough enough to strip the skin. It was not the kind of impression I ever wanted to make on Mother Nature.

Some years in early November the city sent someone to plow the playground close to our house. Almost overnight the playground became the city ice skating rink. For the eager skaters, however, the wait for the ice to freeze tempted their patience beyond resistance. At such times, they approached the rink, placed a foot onto the ice, and heard a crack that broke the ice into jagged lines like summer lighting. Maybe the sound of cracking ice appealed to their aesthetic sensibility, but onomatopoeia will never replace the feel of smooth ice under your skates.

When the water had frozen, neighborhood children converged on the city rink night after night to engage in a game known to children everywhere. Crack the whip. The children joined hands to form a line and then began a pumping motion that gradually accelerated the pace, the steel blades of the skates flaking the ice from the rink. Skaters at the end of the line felt the brunt of the force as the line swung into a circular motion snapping the skaters in whip-like fashion to jar even the sturdiest of spines. If children found it exhilarating, chiropractors might have found it profitable. It was a game with all winners. Afterwards at home, we thawed our cold-bitten fingers and toes in the comfort and warmth of my mother's oven. To dissipate the chill even more, we sipped hot chocolate in cups with marshmallows bobbing over the edges. A cold that had seeped into our very core began to ebb ever so slowly. Hot chocolate may not be a panacea, but as an antidote for winter chill, it's the sweetest cure I know.

While we played our games with a whimsical abandon that was its own joy with no care for any sort of proficiency or skill, the art of figure skating demanded a discipline and practice for those who

preferred the challenge. Shirley Kramer was one of them. While gold medalist Sonja Henie was turning Olympic gold into real currency on the professional skating circuit, Shirley was becoming the closest incarnation of Sonja Henie that Strasburg would ever see. I hadn't the expertise to make an informed assessment of her abilities, but Shirley Kramer, bent with her leg parallel to the ice, cut precise figure eights with an elegance and grace that left potential competitors as only token rivals. I'm not sure if she ever attempted to execute one of those whirling pirouettes that so impress the judges in Oslo, but I judged her just perfect in Strasburg.

Less perfect than those figure eights were the belly landings we executed on the ice with our sleds. We did so like airliners approaching the runway for a landing, the steel runners on our sleds crashing onto the ice to send us headlong across the rink like missiles, sometimes in the path of skaters forced to scuttle themselves to safety. At other times, the Bauer boys and I found a rush of excitement by the railroad tracks on the east edge of town. There we climbed the steep embankments of the tracks, sprinted toward the downward side and flopped our sleds onto the hard-packed snow. That maneuver had the effect of instant acceleration, the whiteness of snow so suddenly upon us our breath seemed to catch in our throats. Those rushes on the tracks, however, seemed but a prelude to an even more daring challenge. The grandstand jump. We put the baseball grandstand on the northwest edge of town to a use never intended by its makers. It became the launching pad for our leaps into space from its roof. Such feats could only be attempted after winter had laid a deep ocean of snow beneath to break our falls. From the roof, we jumped like the intrepid paratroopers we had seen in so many World War II movies, our sudden descent into the white drifts below a free fall into the liberating joy of children at play.

While those snow banks served as our oceans, our imagination also turned them into mountains. Snow banks carved by snow plows adjacent to the convent turned us into aspiring Sir Edmund Hillarys bent on scaling every summit our imaginations could create. The ropes we tied around our waists became a chain of several climbers tethered together in one coordinated unit on a common mission. To scale the heights. It wasn't the sort of challenge that would have daunted Sir Hillary, but for us those mountains of snow were as high as our imaginations made them. Sometimes imagination is enough for children. Adults who value it less may never find mountains to climb.

The passing of Christmas brought more winter games. It was then that we scoured the neighborhoods for discarded Christmas trees. With them we built forts. We did so by hollowing out the snow drift that puffed itself up in the middle of our driveway each winter. That drift was like an uninvited guest. We didn't know what to do with him so we made him part of the fun. After we had hollowed out the middle of the drift, we propped the trees in the snow to form a complete circle that became the ramparts of our fort. Stiff needle-like balsam trees became an impregnable fortification to ward off the Vandals, the Visigoths or the British at Bunker Hill, depending on what scenario we chose to play. The tunnel we dug from the fort gave us access to secret military missions in a night air with a sting that seemed cold enough to pinch the nose from your face. Maybe the accounts of bravery at Valley Forge, stories of hardship and heroism during our nation's fight for independence, stiffened our resolve to carry out the assigned mission. Only the crunching of snow broke the stillness of night as we bellied our way in the snow to ferret out imaginary enemy fortifications. Our ersatz bravery did not go unrecognized. My brother George, who partook in our games, fashioned gaudy colored cardboard medals of Good Conduct and Purple Hearts and pinned them on our chests. None of us would ever become the honored Audie Murphy of World War II, but boys will settle for cardboard heroism until the real thing comes along.

Bright days of winter and games gave way, too, to the dark dangers of winter on the plains. My brother George, perhaps with the fearless naiveté of youth, assumed the chore of delivering the nuns' milk several times a week to the convent. In a less liberated time, the nuns who staffed our schools led a life of relative recluse, removed, except for their duties at school and at church, from the community. The staples of subsistence were often ordered by phone and delivered to the convent. For his service, George was paid fifty cents a month, a paltry amount by current monetary standards, but, at the time, a reasonable sum. George picked up the milk in the early dark of evening on the west edge of town and walked a route of six blocks to the convent. What might have been an uneventful journey took on, for me, the trappings of a gothic tale. For that is when I first heard the dogs of January. In January from the recesses of winter night, the howls of dogs startled my ears. They prickled my spine with a fear and foreboding as if the hound of the Baskervilles had been loosed once again. A more sophisticated sensibility would have dismissed it like a stale device in a hackneyed horror novel, but boys know nothing of trite tales. So I feared for the well-being of my brother. And I feared that I myself might someday find the fangs of those hounds lodged in my throat on another January night. From what pit of darkness they had come, I never knew, but I have not heard their howls in a very long time. Maybe those hounds have returned to the Baskervilles forever. I hope never again to hear their predatory yelps sunder the night.

It should be a common fact that people raised on the plains have a cautious respect for the rage of winter storms. Only the callow recklessness of youth would discard the wisdom of common sense and embark on precarious adventures during winter's wrath. Shortly after Christmas Day many years ago, I and other members of the local independent basketball team, comprised of former high school athletes and anyone who volunteered to play, impulsively decided, despite storm warnings, to keep a game date at Fort Yates. Doing so meant we had to cross the ice-bound Missouri River some twenty miles to the west. That we did so without incident on the way over may have encouraged a foolish hubris that we were invulnerable to the threats of nature. At first, on our return, no one seemed alarmed by the snowflakes dusting the windshield of the car. It wasn't until the dusting turned to drifts and the huge canopy of night fell over us that we felt suddenly small. And frightened. To keep the specter of frostbite at bay, we clapped our hands and stomped our feet while cold and fear tingled us to our very toes. If we had vexed the gods with our impertinent pride, they in turn felt disposed to mercy. Cold that might have dipped to lethal levels seemed stoked in the fires of Hestia's hearth that warmed us just enough to ward off deadly hypothermia. Mythologists may take exception, but I will always be grateful for that Greek goddess of the sacred flame and for Greeks bearing gifts.

Though the gods had granted us a reprieve, calamity struck soon after when snow piled into waves of drifts that no car could navigate. Like a ship at sea, the car began to reel to and fro as if held fast by an unyielding anchor fixing it to the spot. The car was high-centered, anchored in a drift of snow. Since our only recourse was to accelerate in hope of breaking free, maximum pressure was applied to the gas pedal while the driver shifted gears into forward and reverse. Under the hood of the car, the stripping of gears and the gnashing of metal on metal became the throes of a dying transmission while life from the engine sputtered into silence. Our hopes of freeing the car from the drift had suddenly expired. The only sensible option was to pile into one of the other cars and find shelter. Good fortune guided us to a farm house where we prevailed upon its owners to give us refuge from the elements. With morning came daylight and roads passable enough to get us home. We had gambled with stakes much too high on our foolhardy adventure. Transmissions can be replaced. Lives cannot. Still, it took me years to learn that when nature deals the cards, smart players know to fold them before the storm comes.

It is probably true that each generation lays claim to the contention that winters they knew in their childhood were more severe than the current ones. Maybe there's a perverse kind of honor in having survived them, like wearing a Purple Heart that confirms your hardihood. A compelling case can be made for the ones I remember when snow banks almost touched the telephone wires and three-day-howling blizzards blotted out the sun with sheets of snow that stung the skin like projectiles from winter's arsenal. Some of those storms left blue waves of snow in our yard on January nights while I warmed myself on the iron radiators in the living room upstairs in our old house. The iron ridges of those radiators felt like a hot brand. It was also the brand of home and safety and a warmth that no winter could ever cool. But I never forgot how fatal winter can be. Years later during my time in the army on Okinawa, coincidence fired a warning shot. There in *The Stars and Stripes* the account of a young girl who had frozen to death near Strasburg in the March blizzard of 1966 almost felled me like a right cross to the chin. Hestia's fire had gone out.

I will not presume to level a "moral" judgment on the joys or terror of winter. Such verdicts, if necessary at all, are best left to theologians and philosophers. But I prefer to believe that the merry shouts of children on the rink make mute the howling dogs of January and that elegant figures of eight on the ice mark a beauty no fear can efface.

Original Art and Original Photos

Kraft, George
  Page 84, Bell-ringer tolls the bells
  Page 125, Dr. Phibes pounds mad chords on the organ

Kraft, Karla
  Page 11, Easter Bunny
  Page 17, Clock, Lakeside Drive-in
  Page 19, Lakeside Drive-in jukebox & jukebox panel
  Page 53, My thirty-one merit badges
  Page 126, Chandelier at Sts. Peter and Paul's
  Page 127, Stained glass window at Sts. Peter and Paul's
  Page 128, Confessional at Sts. Peter and Paul's
  Page 133, Homemade ice cream
  Page 137, Ice cream freezer
  Page 141, Angels over the Rooftop
  Page 144, Belzanickl makes his rounds
  Page 145, Singing angels

Webskowski, Lisa (Portrait Artist, http://lisawebskowski.com)
  Page 25, Sojourn in the City
  Page 33, The National "Past Time"
  Page 113, "Before the Game"
  Page 118, "Taking the Field"
  Page 151, Winter Bright and Dark

Photo Providers

Duluth News Tribune
> Page 66, NorShor Theater, Duluth, Minnesota

Eckroth, Father Leonard
> Page 36, Father Matthew Fettig, 1948

Emmons County Historical Society, Linton, North Dakota
> Page 121, Strasburg Convent

Frey, Elaine
> Page 57, Stone Lodge at Camp Richmond
> Page 81, Agatha Keller and Pius Kraft

Germans from Russia Heritage Collection
Photographs permission of the Germans from Russia
Heritage Collection, North Dakota State University
Libraries, Fargo (www.ndsu.edu/grhc)
> Page 69, Father Fettig and altar boys
> Page 77, Kraft Brothers Store
> Page 89, Interior of Kraft Brothers Store

Kraft, Bill
> Page 101, Bill and mother Agatha Kraft

Minnesota Historical Society
> Page 29, Forum Cafeteria and Century Theater
> Page 30, Aqua Follies at Theodore Wirth Pool

Previously Published

After the Mall
    Emmons County Record, July 30, 2009

An Altar Boy's Tale of a Tail
    Emmons County Record, April 9, 2009
    Minnesota Moments, January/February 2009

Angels over the Rooftop
    Emmons County Record, December 20, 2007
    Minnesota Moments, November/December 2006

Before the Mall
    Emmons County Record, December 6, 2007
    Minnesota Moments, July/August 2007

Come Back, Van Johnson
    Emmons County Record, April 5, 2007

Echoes of Summer
    Emmons County Record, July 2, 2009
    Minnesota Moments, July/August 2009

A Fever in the Blood
    Minnesota Moments, September/October 2006

Frozen in Time: Homemade Ice Cream
    Emmons County Record, February 21, 2008
    Minnesota Moments, January/February 2008

A Frisson in the Fall
  Emmons County Record, October 30, 2008
  Minnesota Moments, September/October 2008

A Harvest of Memories
  Emmons County Record, October 1, 2009

The Last Merit Badge
  Emmons County Record, May 22, 2008
  Minnesota Moments, July/August 2008

The National "Past Time"
  Emmons County Record, August 2, 2007
  Minnesota Moments, May/June 2007 - alternate title:
  Baseball in a Small Town

Sojourn in the City
  Emmons County Record, May 31, 2007
  Minnesota Moments, July/August 2005

Springtime Has Broken
  Emmons County Record, April 1, 2010

Time Warp in Big Lake
  Minnesota Moments, November/December 2004

Winter Bright and Dark
  Emmons County Record, January 14, 2010
  Minnesota Moments, January/February 2010